THIN RED LINE

Volume 3

**Tracing God's
Amazing Story
of Redemption
Through Scripture**

"THIN RED LINE" SERIES

Thin Red Line, Volume 1
Thin Red Line, Volume 2
Thin Red Line, Volume 3
Thin Red Line, Volume 4

VIDEOS

More New Hope Books by Kimberly Sowell

*Lost on a Familiar Road: Allowing God's Love to
Free Your Mind for the Journey*

Lost on a Familiar Road: eDevotional

Soul Shaping: Creating Compassionate Children

Journey to Confidence: Becoming Women of Influential Faith

Journey to Significance: Becoming Women of Divine Destiny

*Major Truths from the Minor Prophets: Power, Freedom, and Hope for
Women*, coauthors Edna Ellison and Tricia Scribner

A Passion for Purpose: 365 Daily Devotions for Missional Living

Women of the Covenant: Spiritual Wisdom from Women of the Bible

A Month of Miracles: 30 Stories of the Unmistakable Presence of God,
coauthors Edna Ellison, Joy Brown, Tricia Scribner,
Marie Alston, and Cherie Nettles

THIN RED LINE

Volume 3

Tracing God's Amazing Story of Redemption Through Scripture

KIMBERLY
SOWELL

NEW HOPE
PUBLISHERS
Gospel-Centered. Missions-Driven.

BIRMINGHAM, ALABAMA

New Hope® Publishers
PO Box 12065
Birmingham, AL 35202-2065
NewHopeDigital.com
New Hope Publishers is a division of WMU®.

New Hope Publishers serves its authors as they express their views, which
may not express the views of the publisher.

Library of Congress Product Control Number: 2014955637

All Scripture quotations, unless otherwise indicated, are taken from the
New American Standard Bible®, Copyright © 1960, 1962, 1963, 1968,
1971, 1972, 1973, 1975, 1977, 1995 by The Lockman Foundation. Used by
permission.

Scripture quotations marked (NKJV) are taken from the New King James
Version. Copyright © 1982 by Thomas Nelson, Inc. Used by permission. All
rights reserved.

New Hope Publishers series Project Team: Tina Atchenson, Mark Bethea,
Jourdan Berry, Joyce Dinkins, Lynn Groom, Melissa Hall, Joshua Hays, Vicki
Huffman, Maegan Roper, and Kathryne Solomon.

Series cover design: Bruce Watford
Series interior design: Glynese Northam

ISBN: 978-1-59669-432-3
N154111 • 0215 • 2M1

DEDICATION

I wish to dedicate the "Thin Red Line" series to my wonderful church family, Second Baptist Church in Lancaster, South Carolina. Thank you for stepping out in faith as a church to experience God's *thin red line* of redemption together for a year of study. I love you all, and I appreciate your firm stand on the Word of God, your fervent love for Jesus Christ, and your heart that beats for missions. May God continue to bless Second Baptist Church as we move forward to bring glory to His name.

And for each church, Bible study group, and individual who will read this volume and journey along the *Thin Red Line*, may God enrich your walk with Christ and positively flood your heart and mind with His glorious redeeming love.

ACKNOWLEDGMENTS

Every book has its own birth story. The "Thin Red Line" series was born out of my home church's desire to understand fully how all the pieces of the Bible come together to paint one breathtaking picture of redemption. I can tell you that through my personal experience of journeying this *thin red line*, my walk with Christ has been taken to a new level because of my strengthened understanding of what God did to save my soul, and I adore Him all the more. I am excited about what God is going to do in your life and in your church because of this journey you are about to take through redemption's story.

I've tried to go back to the very beginning and retrace the steps of how this book series came into being. I can't remember if it first happened in my office, or my pastor's office; perhaps it was in the executive pastor's office . . . But I remember discussions about the life-changing power of the Word of God. I recall that our hearts were beating rapidly and our voices were escalating with excitement as we began to dream about what could happen if each person in our church began studying together, digging for ourselves to catch the "big picture" of Scripture. We started envisioning the spiritual growth and Bible literacy that God would bring to our people if we started in Genesis and marched through Scripture to thread together the evidence of God's plan from the very beginning—that God would send a Savior to save sin-wrecked humanity.

This church-wide emphasis coupled with the writing process required many people working together for a common purpose to make the "Thin Red Line" series a reality. Our church body embraced this 52-week journey as we studied together. Our weekly Bible study groups studied one lesson per week. Our pastor delivered sermons to reinforce and more fully develop where we were in the timeline as we studied redemption's history together. This was no isolated program; this was the theme of our church for an entire year, and we were blown away with how God transformed us through the power of His Word.

So many people are deserving of thanks:

Dr. Brian Saxon, pastor: Thank you, Pastor Brian, for being willing to take a risk and do something so "out of the box" for the sake of our church family's spiritual growth. Your desire for each person to know and understand God's plan of redemption ushered us to a deeper appreciation for God's great love for all of us.

Marshall Fagg, executive pastor: Preacher Marshall, thank you for helping to shape the vision and develop a format that made this study effective for everyone. Your doctrinal oversight and words of encouragement each week blessed me every step of the way. Whenever you teach God's Word, I am challenged by how deeply you love Jesus Christ.

Denise Johnston, LifeGroup director: Thank you, Denise, for providing leadership to our LifeGroup leaders and paving the way for an out-of-the-ordinary, yet extraordinary year of study. I appreciate your patience and the hard work you put into this process.

Kristie Taylor, editor: Kristie, I knew I could always count on your keen eye and wordsmithing abilities each week. Thank you not only for the editorial input but also the spiritual feedback to sharpen each lesson and encourage me as a writer.

Melanie Sanders, Pat Nobles, and Beth Center, administrative assistants: Thank you for your important role in getting the materials into the hands of our people each week, and always leading with a servant's heart. I appreciate your spirit of cooperation and kindness!

Small-Group Bible Study Leaders: To every leader who accepted the challenge to undergo a shift in how our church experienced small-group Bible studies, thank you for your willingness to stretch, grow, and embrace change. I thank God for the love and leadership that you provide each week as you connect with your small group with the heart of an undershepherd.

The Second Baptist Church Family: Writing this series was my distinct honor because I knew God was allowing me to connect with your lives at a very personal level: your love relationship with Jesus Christ. Thank you for your words of encouragement, your weekly study of God's Word, your celebration of biblical discoveries, and your willingness to live life together with everyone in our church family. I love you very much.

And as always, I want to extend a special thank you to New Hope Publishers team: for your firm commitment to provide Bible study materials that allow the Holy Spirit to be the teacher of each man and woman who opens the Scripture with a willing heart. I love your clarity of vision, and I am honored to partner with you.

CONTENTS

INTRODUCTION

FOLLOW THE SIGNS THAT LEAD TO THE CROSS

What are the Bible stories you remember from childhood? We all have our favorites. Noah's ark. Moses and the bulrushes, Moses and the burning bush, and Moses parting the Red Sea. David and Goliath. Abraham and Isaac. But which story comes first? What is the chronological order? And who was it that fought the battle of Jericho? Where do the judges fit into the Old Testament? When did the prophets come into the picture, and how do they fit into the rest of the Old Testament? When did Israel become a nation, and why is that even important? And can anyone give a clear explanation of how the Old Testament is linked to the New Testament?

If you are one of the blessed individuals who has had exposure to the Bible for much of your life, you could probably sit down with a blank sheet of paper and write down a long list of Bible stories you've studied in your lifetime. You may even be able to jot down a moral or biblical truth to correlate with each story. But so often our Bible study approach can be piecemeal and disjointed, jumping from one text to the next, that we find ourselves possessing an enormous pile of exquisite threads, appreciating each one for its individual beauty, yet unable to weave them together to see the intricate tapestry that is God's big picture.

The "Thin Red Line" series is an opportunity to start at the beginning in the Garden of Eden and walk chronologically through the Bible, tracing the link of commonality found in every book of the Bible: redemption. From beginning to end, God's Word points us to the Cross. The evidence is striking. The benefits reaped from the "Thin Red Line" series are many:

You'll be overwhelmed by God's intentionality. Looking at Scripture passages with one particular focus, God's plan of redemption, will show how He has painstakingly dropped evidence like breadcrumbs through time, leading to the Cross. In fact, throughout this study you'll find that sometimes God left breadcrumbs, but more often He provided large arrows with neon lights pointing people to the promised Savior, His Son, Jesus Christ.

You'll be overwhelmed by God's love. As you study God's master plan and the many ways God interacted with people to usher in their salvation, you cannot help but understand more deeply that humanity is completely undeserving of God's grace. From the beginning God has been consistent, and He has been faithful; you'll see in this study that from the beginning humans are consistently inconsistent and tend toward unfaithfulness. Why did God follow through with the plan? Why did God keep His promise by sending His own Son into this fallen world? It must be love.

You'll grow in Bible literacy. For those who traverse all 52 weeks, you will find a deeper understanding of how the different books of the Bible fit together and how the stories flow chronologically. I confess to you that as the writer, my Bible knowledge grew leaps and bounds as I sat down to march purposefully through time in studying redemption. The growth I experienced has made me a more passionate teacher of God's Word. Whether I'm teaching my children at home around the kitchen table or sharing God's Word in a more formal setting, I long for God's people to possess a working knowledge of the Bible. The "Thin Red Line" series provides a framework for understanding the overall history of Scripture.

You'll fall in love with the Old Testament. It's just a theory, but I believe that many Christians shy away from reading the Old Testament because they don't know the history, they can't figure out the relevance of some of the stories, and they don't see how its contents can deepen their walk with Christ. Prepare to be amazed! You'll fall in love with the Old Testament when you begin to hear its pages whispering the name of Jesus.

You'll fall in love with the New Testament. Follow the "Thin Red Line" series from beginning to end. Your heart is going to sing "glory hallelujah!" when you arrive at the manger, having gained a deeper appreciation for the Babe wrapped in swaddling clothes. When looking through redemption's lens, you'll understand the life of Jesus and the profound nature of every word He said and every act He performed. And how do the Book of Acts and the letters to the churches connect to redemption? Embrace the teachings of *Volume Four* of this series, and experience being a part of God's plan of redemption for all of the peoples of the world.

You'll go to new levels of friendship with your Bible study group. The format of the "Thin Red Line" series lends itself to meaningful, on-topic, highly relevant discussions for your study time together. Each lesson is designed to allow participants to walk away with a solid understanding of the Bible passage (you will remember the details of the story for days to come) and also specific applications from God's Word to put into practice in everyday life. The approach is both discussion-based and Bible-centered.

I pray that God will use this study series to enrich your relationship with Jesus and deepen your love for God's Word. May God's people never cease to be amazed at the grace of God, the Author of our redemption through Jesus Christ!

Kimberly

WELCOME TO THE
THIN RED LINE

Welcome to the *Thin Red Line*. Throughout Scripture, we see a beautiful scarlet thread of God's redemptive plan for humanity. From the beginning, He has implemented a divine strategy to save us from our sins and adopt us as His children. In this study, we will experience powerful life transformation as we understand and embrace how God has revealed Himself and His beautiful redemptive plan from cover to cover in His Holy Word.

Each lesson's small-group leader guide contains some specific components:

RED LINE DETAILS

Red Line Verse: the memory verse for the lesson

Red Line Statement: a statement of how the lesson relates to God's redemptive plan for mankind to be saved

Red Line Connection: the theme of the lesson

Focal Passages: the passages covered in the lesson

Hear—Listen Attentively to the Lesson
This section is the telling of the Bible story and its details from Scripture.

Search—Investigate the Facts of the Lesson

This section examines what is happening in the story, allowing each person to thoroughly digest what is being conveyed in the text. *You'll find group-leader discussion statements in italics.*

See—Find the Purpose of the Lesson

This section allows your small group to begin processing what God is teaching about Himself and how they can live for Him. Your group will discuss the significance of God's truths and how they apply to their lives. *You'll find group-leader discussion statements in italics.*

Live—Experience the Truth of the Lesson

This section is a crucial component of the lesson—sharing how God's Word is reshaping your hearts and minds to be strong disciples of Jesus Christ. In this section that closes each lesson, you will have the opportunity as the small-group leader to challenge your group to respond specifically and to implement this lesson in their lives the following week. *See discussion statements in italics.*

THE KING OF GLORY

Lift up your heads, O gates,
And be lifted up, O ancient doors,
That the King of glory may come in!
Who is the King of glory?
The LORD STRONG AND MIGHTY,
The LORD MIGHTY IN BATTLE.
LIFT UP YOUR HEADS, O GATES,
And lift them up, O ancient doors,
That the King of glory may come in!
Who is this King of glory?
The LORD OF HOSTS,
He is the King of glory.
—PSALM 24:7-10

He is grace unspeakable. He is wisdom unfathomable. He is peace unexplainable. He is love like the world has never known. He was, is, and is to come. Jesus is the King of Glory.

God sent His Son not as an act of desperation, a "Plan B" to rescue men and women from their own evil. God sent the Messiah not on a whim—a passing thought that the world needed a fresh voice or another good teacher. No, for the *thin red line* of God's redemption appeared in the volume of human history on page one, where God promised a Seed to defeat Satan (Genesis 3:15). And that crimson thread ran through many a prophet's words, many a foreshadowing in ancient days, until God declared that the time had come to fulfill His promise of a Savior. The Savior Jesus arrived on the dusty earth in the same way He would depart in death, most humbly. And yet, His radiant glory lit His path from the manger to the Cross.

LIFE LESSON 27

THE BIRTH OF OUR LORD

Red Line Verse: *"She will bear a Son; and you shall call His name Jesus, for He will save His people from their sins."* (Matthew 1:21)

Red Line Statement: God's promises are fulfilled in Jesus Christ, the Messiah, who came to save us from our sins.

Red Line Connection: In times past, God sent human deliverers and leaders to rescue His people from their enemies; when God sent His Son, He sent the ultimate Deliverer. Jesus sets us free from the power of sin.

Background Passage: Matthew 1–2

Focal Passage: Matthew 1:18–2:12

 Listen Attentively to the Lesson

1. Tell the story of Matthew 1:18–2:12 in your own words.

   Context: When the Northern and Southern Kingdoms were conquered, the prophets spoke to the Jews about judgment along with deliverance, and their history along with their future. God reminded His people of the covenants between them and that the ultimate fulfillment of these promises was coming. After the ministry of the prophets ceased (Malachi in our Bibles), there came 400 years of silence. When Jesus came, the silence was broken. Briefly highlight Matthew 1:1–17 with your small group. Perhaps more than ever before, your small-group members will appreciate the lineage of Christ as they read through names they studied in Volumes 1 and 2 of *Thin Red Line*. This lineage reinforces to us that the birth of Jesus is not an isolated event in human history, as some in the world might say. Jesus wasn't just another great teacher who arrived on the scene and captivated people's attention. Jesus is the fulfillment of God's plan from the beginning and specifically the fulfillment of the original covenant God made with Abraham.

2. Ask the small-group members to reconstruct the story of Matthew 1:18–2:12 together, including as many details as they can remember.

3. Read the passage aloud together from Scripture, confirming the facts of the story. Amend any details suggested by small-group members that did not accurately represent the Scripture.

 Investigate the Facts of the Lesson
Use these questions to guide small-group members to investigate the facts of this passage.

1. How does Matthew 1:18 show us that Jesus was both fully God and fully man?

    Jesus was born of the virgin Mary in the natural way, but the Holy Spirit had conceived this Child.

2. How would you describe the character of Joseph?

    He had the legal right to have Mary publically stoned because of the pregnancy (Deuteronomy 22:13–21), but he was not planning to humiliate and punish her. Joseph showed compassion toward Mary and also courage to accept the responsibility to raise Jesus in his home.

3. The birth of Jesus had been foretold in many ways and throughout human history.

a. Who especially should have been looking for the arrival of the Messiah?

The Jews above all should have been looking for the One God had promised them.

b. Who came looking for the Messiah in this passage (2:1–2)?

The wise men (or magi) from the East were looking for Jesus in order to worship Him. They called Him the King of the Jews, and they first came to Jerusalem, the city where God had chosen to place His name (1 Kings 11:36). The wise men were Gentiles, probably astrologers.

c. Whom did King Herod consult about this King of the Jews? Who actually went to Bethlehem to find the Christ Child (2:4–9)?

Herod consulted the chief priests and scribes, the religious leaders of the Jews. However, note that this visit from the wise men didn't prompt the chief priests and scribes to travel the five miles from Jerusalem to Bethlehem to see Christ for themselves. Why weren't they interested in going to Bethlehem too? Why didn't they want to worship their King?

4. What are the names ascribed to the Baby born to Mary in this passage (1:18, 21, 23; 2:2, 4, 6)?

He is Jesus, which means Savior, from the Hebrew name Joshua ("Jehovah is salvation"). He is Immanuel, "God with us" (Isaiah 7:14). He is the King of the Jews. He is a Ruler who shepherds Israel. He is the Christ ("anointed" and the Greek equivalent to "Messiah").

5. What other details do you see in this passage?

Allow your small group to share other details that stand out to them and discuss the significance of each point.

Find the purpose of the lesson

Use these questions to guide small-group members to discover God's purpose for the passage.

1. When the angel appeared to Joseph, he addressed Joseph's fears first. What were the possible fears that Joseph was experiencing? When does God have to remind you not to fear?

Allow your small group to share their personal experiences.

Possible answers: Joseph may have feared that Mary would prove to be an unfaithful bride who would bring heartache and humiliation to his life. Perhaps Joseph feared making the wrong decision that would affect his future. Joseph may have feared the unknown. Even Mary and the shepherds, when they heard the news about Jesus, were also first told, "Do not be afraid" (Luke 1:30; 2:10). God knows when we're afraid, and He encourages us to trust Him.

2. Herod was "troubled" by news of the birth of the King of the Jews, and Jerusalem suffered the repercussions of his troubled mind (2:3). Why are people today still troubled by the idea of Jesus being King? How does their troubled attitude spill out on the people around them?

King Jesus deserves our worship and to rule over our lives. We are subject to His authority. Those who rebel against His sovereignty want to rule and reign over themselves. Their rebellious spirit often results in their wielding a negative influence over others. Discuss with your small group the blessings that come from bowing to Christ's authority.

3. Which prophecies of Jesus do we see fulfilled in this passage? Why is this important?

Jesus is the fulfillment of God's promises to Abraham and David (1:1–17); Jesus was born of a virgin (1:23); Christ was born in Bethlehem (2:6).

If time permits, briefly share how the angel warned Joseph to take Jesus to Egypt (2:15), fulfilling Hosea 11:1, and that Herod ordered the death of all males ages two and under in Bethlehem and surrounding districts (2:16), fulfilling Jeremiah 31:15. Later Joseph moved the family to Nazareth (2:23). The fulfillment of prophecies is a gift from God to strengthen our belief in Jesus as the Christ.

4. Matthew 2:11 is a beautiful picture of how we interact with Christ.

a. In this one verse, how did the wise men show humility? Faith? Sacrifice? Adoration?

(Your small group may choose other words to describe what the wise men experienced.)

Possible answers—humility: they fell down before the Christ Child. Faith: they worshipped Him. They believed that He was the Christ, worthy of more than simple allegiance to a king but also worship as God. Sacrifice: based on Matthew 2:7 and 16, the wise men had probably been traveling for at least several months to reach the King of the Jews. These were wealthy men of position who chose to leave the comforts of home and travel a great distance to meet Jesus. Adoration: they brought gifts worthy of a King.

b. They brought gold, frankincense, and myrrh. What gifts do you bring to Jesus?

Discuss the gifts that Christ desires of His followers.

c. Between humility, faith, sacrifice, or adoration, which of these acts is your favorite expression of worship before God? Why?

Allow your small group to respond, and be prepared to share from your own lifestyle of worship. Help your small group think of ways they can daily express humility, faith, sacrifice, and adoration before the Lord.

5. What other truths from this passage stand out to you? What else can we learn about God or learn about being a follower of Christ?

Allow everyone to respond. Share any other points of spiritual growth that the Holy Spirit brings to your attention.

Experience the Truth of the Lesson

Use these questions to guide small-group members to allow God's transformational truths to reshape their hearts and minds.

1. How do we know that God wanted the wise men to find Jesus (2:2, 9)? How did God lead you to find Jesus Christ for yourself? How did you "rejoice" the way the wise men rejoiced when they saw the star (2:10)?

God was the One who placed the star in the sky to guide them to the Savior. We might also say that only God could work in their hearts to give the wise men the desire to travel such a great distance not only to meet the King of the Jews, but also to worship Him as God. Allow your small group to share their stories of how God led them to meet Jesus.

2. Jesus was unlike any other deliverer or king that God had provided for the Jews. Think about what you've learned about the deliverers of Israel (Moses, Joshua, the judges, and the kings) and what you know about the life and teachings of Jesus. How was Jesus set apart as the ultimate Deliverer for the Jews? How is Jesus the Deliverer in your life?

Possible answers: Jesus did not come to help the Jews defeat their enemies in battle; instead, Jesus said to love our enemies (Luke 6:35). Jesus wasn't reestablishing God's people in the Promised Land of Canaan, but He came to reestablish us in a new promised land, Heaven (John 14:2–4). Jesus came to offer complete freedom from the oppression of evil and sin, not freedom from the burden of worldly oppressors (John 8:36).

3. This story could be told from many different perspectives—that of Mary and Joseph, the wise men, Herod the King, or the chief priests and scribes. Who has the most tragic role in this story? Who has the most blessed role?

   Be prepared to share your own answers.

Between the Lines: Truth Points

Betrothed (1:18)—the betrothal period before marriage between a Hebrew man and woman was a time of covenant. During the betrothal, the man and woman were legally bound to one another as in marriage, but the two would not be considered married until their relationship was consummated.

Son of David (1:20)—Matthew 1:1–17 traces the lineage of Jesus, which includes King David and includes Joseph, the earthly stepfather of Jesus.

Bethlehem (2:1)—means "house of bread"; Jesus is the Bread of Life (John 6:48).

Herod the King (2:1)—Herod the Great was appointed King of the Jews by Augustus. He was known for his cruelty, but he also attempted to appease the Jews by reconstructing the Temple.

Magi (2:1)—a term used to described educated men who were considered scientists, astrologers, or workers of magic.

Frankincense (2:11)—an ingredient used to make the perfume for the Most Holy Place in the tent of meeting (Exodus 30:34–36).

Myrrh (2:11)—an ingredient used to make anointing oil (Exodus 30:22–33). Myrrh was used for its pleasant aroma (Esther 2:12; Psalm 45:8) and for embalming (John 19:39).

The star of Bethlehem was a star of hope that led the wise men to the fulfillment of their expectations, the success of their expedition. Nothing in this world is more fundamental for success in life than hope, and this star pointed to our only source for true hope: Jesus Christ. D. JAMES KENNEDY

FOLLOWING THE EXAMPLE OF JESUS

Red Line Verse: *"Why is it that you were looking for Me? Did you not know that I had to be in My Father's house?"* (Luke 2:49)

Red Line Statement: Jesus came to fulfill the will of His Father and, even as a youth, He remained focused on His calling.

Red Line Connection: Jesus Christ willingly came to the earth to give His entire life in sacrifice for us according to God's perfect plan.

Focal Passage: Luke 2:40–52

 Listen Attentively to the Lesson

1. Tell the story of Luke 2:40–52 in your own words.

    Context: Little is known about the childhood of Jesus. Today's Scripture passage is a rare opportunity to peer into the family life of young Jesus and to consider the interactions He had with Mary and Joseph. While this story has often been taught in isolation from the whole of the life of Christ, putting this story in the context of the *thin red line* helps us to understand at least one reason why God gives us this glimpse into Jesus' life as a youth. Even as a child, Jesus had a desire to fulfill His calling and obey the will of His Father.

2. Reconstruct Luke 2:40–52 together, including as many details as your small group remembers.

3. Read the passage aloud together from Scripture, confirming the facts of the story. Amend any details suggested by small-group members that did not accurately represent the Scripture.

Investigate the Facts of the Lesson

Use these questions to guide small-group members to investigate the facts of this passage.

1. When and where did this event occur (v. 41)? What is the significance of this celebration?

   They were in Jerusalem at the time of the Feast of the Passover, which was first instituted when God sent the tenth plague (death of the firstborn) upon Egypt (Exodus 12:1–28). The Passover Feast celebrated God's deliverance from bondage and death, and included the death of a lamb without spot or blemish. Jesus Himself would be the perfect Lamb of God who would deliver us from bondage and death. The Feast of the Passover will be significant again when Jesus celebrates the Last Supper with His disciples in Jerusalem (Life Lesson 36).

2. How did Jesus get separated from Mary and Joseph (vv. 43–44)?

   Traveling with extended family and friends, or even as a village, was common in this culture. Mary and Joseph assumed that Jesus was among their caravan of travelers.

3. What were the emotions that Mary and Joseph experienced in this passage?

> *Discuss the feeling of a parent when a child is lost, which Mary described as an anxious search (v. 48). They also experienced astonishment (v. 48), confusion (v. 50), and a sense of wonder or contemplation for Mary (v. 51).*

4. What was Jesus doing in Jerusalem (v. 46)? Why were the people astonished (v. 47)?

> *Jesus was dialoging with the teachers in the Temple. They were astonished at His understanding and His answers.*

5. What other details do you see in this passage?

> *Allow your small group to share other details that stand out to them and discuss the significance of each point.*

 Find the purpose of the lesson

Use these questions to guide small-group members to discover God's purpose for the passage.

1. Jesus was only 12 when this event occurred (v. 42). The Temple leaders weren't expecting a youth to be capable of such depths of understanding.

    a. How old were you when an understanding of God became a priority in your life?

    > *Allow your small group to respond.*

    b. Do you consider it a normal part of the Christian life to search out the wisdom of God, or do you find it astonishing and remarkable when you meet someone who passionately seeks God?

As people respond, help small-group members realize that their personal expectations can have a major impact on their own walk with Christ as well as the walk of the people around them. When our expectations are low and we believe that only "especially called" people live that kind of lifestyle, we won't search for God with diligence and we won't encourage others to live for Christ. When we begin to believe that every Christian can have a deep understanding of the things of God, we will seek God with a passion and will naturally nudge our loved ones to join us on this quest to know God.

2. Jesus was fully God and fully man, and here we see the young Jesus being teachable. He carved out time to listen, ask questions, and discuss the things of God.

    a. What must take place in our hearts to make us teachable?
        Possible answers: humility; a thirst for knowledge; a maturity to respect those who have knowledge that we don't yet have; curiosity, and interest.

    b. What are your personal challenges to being deeply interested in the things of God?
        Be willing to share honestly about your own personal struggles. As your small group shares issues of time constraints, mental fatigue, or other personal challenges, don't end the discussion with the challenges. Ask your small group to meet each challenge with a solution.

3. When Mary asked Jesus about what happened, Jesus responded with two questions (v. 49).

    a. How does Jesus' response show that He was aware of His identity as the Son of God?
        Jesus called God His Father, and Jesus realized that He was on the earth to do His Father's will or "business" (NKJV).

b. How did Jesus' actions match His calling?

> *Jesus was growing in knowledge and preparing Himself to fulfill His call-ing. (This concept may be difficult for some to grasp, that the Son of God was gaining knowledge, but Luke 2:52 indicates that Jesus experienced growth.)*

c. How do your actions match your calling?

> *Allow everyone to respond. Are they aware of their calling? Are they fulfilling the call?*

4. Mary and Joseph were astonished by Jesus (v. 48), and they didn't understand (v. 50). Should they have understood? Who else was close to Jesus but also misunderstood Him?

> *No one was as close to Jesus during His childhood as Mary and Joseph, yet they struggled to understand who He was. Your small-group members may have different ideas about how much Mary and Joseph should have understood, because they both had been given individual instruction through an angel about the identity of Jesus before His birth. However, the disciples also often misunderstood Jesus during their days of ministry. Ask your small group to be encouraged and not discouraged by Mary and Joseph's lack of understanding. God was patient with them. Despite their human limitations, God gave them the privilege to watch over the growth of Jesus. God is patient with us too. We must keep moving forward in obedience to God.*

5. Mary tucked this experience in her heart, much like her response when the shepherds came at Jesus' birth (2:19). How do you hold onto the truths God teaches you in the moments of your life? Do you allow yourself time to ponder your experiences and hear God's voice?

> *Encourage your small group to value the importance of learning each lesson God teaches them through life experiences. Challenge them to invest time to think, reflect, and pray.*

6. What other truths from this passage stand out to you? What else can we learn about God or learn about being a follower of Christ?

   Allow everyone to respond. Share any other points of spiritual growth that the Holy Spirit brings to your attention.

Experience the Truth of the Lesson

Use these questions to guide small-group members to allow God's transformational truths to reshape their hearts and minds.

1. How would your life change if you followed the example of Jesus and invested more time seeking a deeper understanding of God?

   Such a question warrants giving your small group a moment to sit still and seek the answer from God. Give everyone a moment, and then challenge each person to give a specific answer. Encourage them to "dream big" about how purposeful and fulfilling their life journeys could be if they went deeper in their walk with Christ. Then ask, "Is there anything stopping you from making this life adjustment?"

2. With so little of Jesus' childhood recorded in Scripture, we must consider that God had a specific purpose in sharing this story with us. How does this story connect with God's plan of redemption on the *thin red line*?

   Possible answer: God's plan has always been to send His Son to be our Savior. Jesus' self-awareness at such a young age gives us deeper insight into His passion, purpose, and sense of urgency for being obedient even unto death on the Cross (Philippians 2:8).

3. Luke 2:52 is a summary of Jesus' childhood, and it's a great formula for life. What did Jesus value in His growth? How can you stay balanced in your personal growth to live more like Jesus?

Jesus grew mentally, spiritually, and physically, and He grew in His relationships both with God and with people. Ask your small group to discuss the blessings of well-rounded growth and meaningful relationships. Ask them to allow God to work in any areas they have been neglecting. Pray that each of you will value what God has called valuable.

Between the Lines: Truth Points

Feast of the Passover (v. 41)—the first of the three annual festivals of the Jews. The animal to be slain was selected on the tenth day of the month and killed on the fourteenth day, then eaten (Exodus 12:3, 6). This feast was also called the Feast of Unleavened Bread because unleavened bread was to be eaten for seven days after Passover (Exodus 13:6–7; 23:15).

Caravan (v. 44)—a group of travelers who journeyed together for safety or comfort.

Nazareth (v. 51)—a small village in lower Galilee. Jesus was often named in association with this city of His childhood, being called "Jesus of Nazareth"; when Jesus appeared to Saul (Paul), He also identified Himself as "Jesus the Nazarene" (Acts 22:8).

We spend our lives dreaming of the future, not realizing that a little of it slips away every day.   Barbara Johnson

32

TEMPTED YET VICTORIOUS

Red Line Verse: *For we do not have a high priest who cannot sympathize with our weaknesses, but One who has been tempted in all things as we are, yet without sin.* (Hebrews 4:15)

Red Line Statement: Jesus took on flesh and faced temptation, but He was victorious over temptation and remained without sin.

Red Line Connection: Jesus can sympathize with our struggles with temptation because He, too, was tempted. His victory gives us hope that we can also be victorious over sin.

Focal Passage: Luke 4:1–13

 Listen Attentively to the Lesson

1. Tell the story of Luke 4:1–13 in your own words.

    Context: Jesus was about 30 years old when He began His earthly ministry (3:23). After Jesus was baptized by John the Baptist, He was led by the Spirit into the wilderness to be tempted by the devil (Matthew 3:13–4:1).

2. Reconstruct Luke 4:1–13 together, including as many details as your small group remembers.

3. Read the passage aloud together from Scripture, confirming the facts of the story. Amend any details suggested by small-group members that did not accurately represent the Scripture.

 Investigate the Facts of the Lesson
Use these questions to guide small-group members to investigate the facts of this passage.

1. Why was Jesus in a physically weakened state (v. 2)?

    He hadn't eaten for forty days. The devil tries to take advantage of our times of weakness.

2. Where did the temptations take place (vv. 1–2, 5, 9)?

    Jesus was tempted in the wilderness, on a high mountain, and on the pinnacle of the Temple in Jerusalem.

3. What weapon did Jesus use to defeat the devil? Where did His words come from?

    Jesus quoted Scripture to defeat the devil. Jesus quoted three passages from Deuteronomy, when Moses gave final commands to the Children of Israel before they entered the Promised Land. These were the children of the Israelites who had wandered for 40 years in the wilderness because of their lack of faith in God. Jesus was now in the wilderness for 40 days, experiencing some of the temptations they had faced, like hunger (Deuteronomy 8:3, quoted in Luke 4:4); turning from full faith in God alone (Deuteronomy 6:13, quoted in Luke 4:8); and tempting God (Deuteronomy 6:16, quoted in Luke 4:12). Deuteronomy 6:16 refers to a time when the Israelites were thirsty and complained, "Is the LORD among us or not" (Exodus 17:7)?

4. What other details do you see in this passage?

Allow your small group to share other details that stand out to them and discuss the significance of each point.

Find the purpose of the lesson

Use these questions to guide small-group members to discover God's purpose for the passage.

1. The first temptation was for Jesus to turn the stone into bread (vv. 3–4).

   a. Jesus was hungry. Why wouldn't Jesus do what the devil suggested?

      Possible answer: In Jesus' answer, He focused on the Word of God. His Father hadn't instructed Him to get food in this manner, and Jesus would not use His power to do what His Father hadn't permitted Him to do. Jesus would not end His fast until His Father said it was time. Jesus knew His Father would meet His needs at the proper time.

   b. You also have needs that are real and legitimate. Read James 1:14–17 carefully. How can we be deceived when we focus on our own needs and desires? All of our good and perfect gifts come from God. How does this truth help us resist the temptation to seize our own provision?

      We can be deceived by the devil when we focus on our desires and needs instead of focusing on God our Provider. Knowing that He will supply all of our needs gives us the faith to be still and wait upon His provision. We are never justified to compromise our morals or faith, because God is faithful to meet all our needs.

2. The second temptation: the devil offered Jesus the world's kingdoms in exchange for worship (vv. 5–8).

   a. How was the devil deceptive in what he promised Jesus in verse 6?

   God has ultimate authority, and the devil only has the loose rein that God has granted him for a season. Jesus would gain nothing from rebelling against His Father to worship Satan.

   b. The devil said, "If You worship before me, it shall all be Yours" (v. 7). How does he tempt people today with this same empty promise? How would you fill in the blank for Satan's common lies that people fall for: "If you will _____, all will be yours"?

   Allow everyone to respond, and be prepared to share your own answers.

   c. This temptation began with the devil flashing all of the kingdoms before Jesus' eyes. How does Satan continue to use this tactic today, flashing temptations before our eyes?

   Possible answers: media, advertising, pornography, revealing clothing, displays of wealth.

   d. The devil offered Jesus an "easy" route to become king, but Jesus knew He had to suffer and die as the King of glory. Later in His ministry when Jesus told His disciples that He would have to suffer and die, Peter disagreed with Jesus, and Jesus faced this same issue of temptation; Jesus then also said to Peter, "Get behind Me, Satan!" (Matthew 16:23). Read Matthew 16:23–26. Jesus faced this temptation first from the devil, and then from His friend, Peter. Have you ever faced the same temptation several times and from various sources? How can you maintain consistency to resist temptation every time?

Help your small group recognize Jesus' consistency—He was willing to suffer and die to honor the Father's will, and He let no one dissuade Him. Discuss whether temptations have a stronger pull on us when they're suggested by family or friends. We must be wise in our associations, but more importantly, we must also be firmly resolved that we will obey God.

3. The third temptation was for Jesus to throw Himself from the Temple pinnacle (vv. 9–12).

   a. What was the source of the devil's words in Luke 4:11–12? Does that surprise you?

      The devil quoted Scripture. He was mishandling God's Word. Discuss how "wolves in sheep's clothing" deceive people by misusing Scripture. What is the warning for us?

   b. If Satan can quote Scripture, how can we defend against his lies?

      Ephesians 6:17 teaches us that the armor of God includes the sword of the Spirit, which is the Word of God. We must study the Scripture under the Holy Spirit's leadership (John 16:13), and allow the Holy Spirit to guide us.

   c. How would throwing Himself from the Temple have been an act of Jesus tempting God?

      Possible answer: Jesus would have been stepping out of His Father's will to try to force God to respond in rescue.

4. Twice the devil began by saying, "If You are the Son of God . . ." (v. 3, 9).

   a. Why would this phrase potentially heighten the temptations the devil threw before Jesus?

The devil knew that Jesus was God's Son, but his words showed disrespect and were possibly an attempt to provoke Jesus to respond out of pride. People may use this same tactic to try to force us to do what they want us to do ("Since you're such a good husband, why don't you..."; "If you're the respected employee that you say you are, why don't you..."; "If you're such a good Christian, why don't you..."). We have to battle the pride of our flesh and reject the temptation to prove ourselves to others. Giving in to such tactics only gives the other person control over us, leaving us vulnerable because we're not under the control of the Holy Spirit.

b. Jesus was sure of His identity as the Son of God. How does our self-perception factor into our strength to withstand temptation?

Allow your small group to respond. You may discuss the many ways in which moral failures can be linked to a person's low self-worth. God's aim is not for us to exalt ourselves, but that we exalt Him by living as children of God who understand and value who we are in Christ. Allow your small group to explore the importance of embracing our identity in Christ. We can also be vulnerable to sins of omission because of low self-worth, if we choose not to serve Him because we don't believe we're capable of being used by God.

5. In Matthew's account of this event, the angels ministered to Jesus after the devil left (Matthew 4:11). How have spiritual battles affected you lately? How can God use fellow Christians to encourage and minister to you? Do you allow people to know about your spiritual needs?

Be prepared to share from your personal experiences. Discuss how your small group can be a safe place for the sharing of burdens, and how God has designed us as the body of Christ to encourage and minister to one another.

6. What other truths from this passage stand out to you? What else can we learn about God or learn about being a follower of Christ?

Allow everyone to respond. Share any other points of spiritual growth that the Holy Spirit brings to your attention.

Experience the Truth of the Lesson

Use these questions to guide small-group members to allow God's transformational truths to reshape their hearts and minds.

1. As we read the Gospels, we realize that only a limited number of Jesus' life stories are recorded, while thousands of others weren't chosen by God to be placed in Scripture. Why this story? Read Hebrews 4:15. How does knowing that Jesus faced these temptations encourage you in your battle against sin? What does this passage teach us about the nature of temptation?

   What a joy to know that Jesus can sympathize with our battle against temptations because He has also experienced temptation. Because Jesus experienced temptation, it assures us that feeling tempted is not a sin; it's only when we yield to temptation that we fall into sin. And because Jesus overcame temptation and remained sinless, we are encouraged to know we can also have victory through Jesus Christ (Romans 6:6).

2. James 4:7 teaches us to "resist the devil and he will flee from you," just as he finally departed from Jesus (v. 13). How has this study prepared you to resist temptation this week?

   Encourage everyone to share, and emphasize Jesus' example of how to face temptation.

Between the Lines: Truth Points

Jordan (v. 1)—the place of Jesus' baptism (3:21).

Domain and glory (v. 6)—Jesus called Satan the ruler of this world (John 12:31, 14:30). God has "handed" authority to Satan (v. 6), but God reigns supreme and Satan's defeat is certain (Hebrews 2:14; 1 John 3:8).

Pinnacle (v. 9)—the highest point of the Temple structure. Scholars are not certain about where the pinnacle was located in the architectural design of the Temple.

The devil's use of Scripture (vv. 10–11)—he quoted Psalm 91:11–12, but he omitted the last phrase of verse 11: "to guard you in all your ways."

You who have yielded so readily to your friend's persuasion and have joined him in doing wrong, you know not how many times a very little resistance would have saved both him and yourself. You know not how many times he was hesitating already and would have drawn back altogether if you had but given him an opening to do so. You know not how often at the very time he was arguing with you, he was in reality arguing against his own conscience and might have been turned back with ease if you had not given way.   FREDERICK TEMPLE

LIFE LESSON 30

Jesus Calls Us to Serve Him

- **Red Line Verse:** *Philip found Nathanael and said to him, "We have found Him of whom Moses in the Law and also the Prophets wrote—Jesus of Nazareth, the son of Joseph."* (John 1:45)

- **Red Line Statement:** Jesus invested particularly in the lives of 12 men, training them to be disciples of Christ and to make disciples of others.

- **Red Line Connection:** Each of us who follow Christ have a role to play on God's thin red line of redemption as we serve as disciples and we make disciples for Christ.

- **Focal Passage:** John 1:35–51

 Listen Attentively to the Lesson

1. Tell the story of John 1:35–51 in your own words.

   Context: One of the first things Jesus did when He began His earthly ministry was assemble His team of disciples. John the Baptist had been on the scene, baptizing people in the River Jordan and preparing Israel to receive their Messiah (1:31). John had disciples, but he knew that Jesus was the Son of God, and the attention needed to shift to Christ. John said, "He must increase, but I must decrease" (3:30). Jesus' disciples would play a role in this process, as Jesus mentored and poured His life into these 12 men.

2. Reconstruct John 1:35–51 together, including as many details as your small group remembers.

3. Read the passage aloud together from Scripture, confirming the facts of the story. Amend any details suggested by small-group members that did not accurately represent the Scripture.

Investigate the Facts of the Lesson

Use these questions to guide small-group members to investigate the facts of this passage.

1. When Jesus asked two of John the Baptist's disciples what they were seeking, what was their response (v. 38)? What were they seeking?

   The disciples responded by asking Jesus where He was staying, which wasn't an answer to Jesus' question. Perhaps they wanted to have plenty of time to talk with Jesus. Allow your small group to think through what these two men were looking for when they followed Jesus.

2. When Jesus changed Simon Peter's name, how could this have encouraged him (v. 42)? What does Peter's name signify?

   The meaning of one's name carried great significance in Hebrew culture, and God had changed the names of others in the past when He connected with their lives (for example, Abraham, Sarah, and Jacob). Jesus took note of Simon Peter enough to give him the new name "stone" or "rock."

3. How does Jesus' invitation in verse 39 compare to His invitation in verse 43? In verse 46, how do Philip's words indicate that he was already learning from Christ?

Both of Jesus' invitations let the men know that He wanted to take them somewhere, and that He would go with them. Philip borrowed Jesus' words when he invited Nathanael to "come and see" (v. 46). Christ followers follow Jesus in word and deed.

4. Study Philip's description of Messiah (v. 45). How do his words compare to what we have also been studying about the promised Messiah?

   Philip pointed Nathanael to the Old Testament's prophecies and promises. Philip was aware of God's thin red line of redemption that would come through Jesus.

5. What other details do you see in this passage?

   Allow your small group to share other details that stand out to them and discuss the significance of each point.

43

Find the purpose of the lesson
Use these questions to guide small-group members to discover God's purpose for the passage.

1. John the Baptist was pouring his life into a group of men to help them develop spiritually; he was discipling them to become disciples of Jesus (vv. 35–37). Each of us has the same privilege to develop relationships with people to encourage them to live for Christ. Think about your circle of friends whom you influence. Are you pointing people to know and follow Christ?

   As small-group members consider their responses, help them explore their answers by asking them how they influence their friends for Christ. How do they know if people are living for Christ because of their influence?

2. In verse 38, Jesus asked a critical question: "What do you seek?" How would you answer that question in this season of your life? What are you really seeking?

Allow your small group to share. Encourage them to explore the answer to this question based on their investment of time and money, how they spend their leisure time, their preferred source for answers and life direction, the focus of their thought life, etc.

3. Why did the men in this passage follow Jesus? Why do you follow Jesus?

Possible answers: They were looking for the Messiah, and God helped them recognize that Jesus was His Son. Why we follow Christ is a question we should each be ready to answer for our own benefit as well as for the benefit of the people we meet who need to be introduced to our Savior.

4. This passage contains three examples of followers of Christ being used by God to develop more followers of Christ.

   a. In the case of John the Baptist (vv. 35–36), Andrew (v. 41), and Philip (v. 45), whom did they approach?

   John spoke to his disciples, Andrew spoke to his brother, and Philip spoke to his friend. They approached people with whom they had a relationship. Their example isn't a directive to share Christ only with friends and family, but a clear principle arises that shows us the value of approaching people with whom we have developed a relationship.

   b. John, Andrew, and Philip each had a conversation about spiritual matters, and they were specifically talking about Jesus. Is it necessary to bring up Jesus in order for a conversation to be "spiritual"? How often do you have spiritual conversations with your family? Your friends?

John called Jesus the Lamb of God, Andrew called Him Messiah, and Philip called Him the fulfillment of the law and prophets. "There is no other name under heaven which has been given among men by which we may be saved" (Acts 4:12). Talking about spiritual matters is important, but talking about Jesus is vital. Spirituality has no meaning apart from Jesus.

c. Andrew brought his brother, Simon Peter, to Jesus (v. 42). Who brought you to Jesus? Whom are you bringing to Jesus?

Encourage your small group to pray for one another with great intentionality about the people you're desiring to bring to Christ.

5. Nathanael was amazed that Jesus knew him, but Jesus let Nathanael know that he was going to be continually amazed at what his eyes would see (vv. 48–50). Nathanael's scope had to become bigger than just his personal connection with Christ. Is it important to try to know about the work of God beyond your own life? How do you grow in awareness of the amazing things God is doing in your community, nation, and around the world?

Ask your small group to share how their walk with Christ is affected when they learn about how God has worked in the life of another person or even how He's working in the world.

6. Read John 2:23–25. What was the difference between the men described in this passage and men like John the Baptist, Andrew, Simon Peter, Philip, and Nathanael?

Jesus didn't commit Himself to these men in John 2:23–25, even though they believed in His name. Jesus "knew what was in man" (v. 25). Were these men who saw the signs willing to be disciples of Jesus? Discuss.

7. What other truths from this passage stand out to you? What else can we learn about God or learn about being a follower of Christ?

Allow everyone to respond. Share any other points of spiritual growth that the Holy Spirit brings to your attention.

 Experience the Truth of the Lesson

Use these questions to guide small-group members to allow God's transformational truths to reshape their hearts and minds.

What is the vision God wants to give your small group as you study this passage of Scripture? John the Baptist pointed his disciples to be followers of Christ, and Andrew and Philip also brought people from their circles of friends and family to be followers of Jesus. John, Andrew, and Philip understood what it meant to be disciples of Christ who make more disciples of Christ under the leadership of the Lord (Matthew 28:18–20).

Take a moment to consider the possibilities for your small group:

1. If our small group followed the example of Andrew and Philip, inviting friends and family to "come and see" who Jesus is, how would this change the look and feel of our small group? Would it change the focus of our small group?

2. When Andrew and Philip brought Simon Peter and Nathanael to Jesus, the Lord did not disappoint; Jesus revealed Himself to Simon Peter and Nathanael, and He transformed their lives. If our small group began to regularly introduce people to Jesus, what is your expectation of what Jesus would do in your friends' and family members' lives?

3. John the Baptist pointed all of his disciples to follow Jesus. How can our small group and small-group leaders guard against making followers of the small group instead of followers of Christ?

4. When John the Baptist completed the task of developing his group of men, He released them to follow their own callings. Their bonds of friendship and their group was forever changed. In what ways would that have been difficult for those men and for John? What good came from that change? As a group of people who dearly love one another, how does our small group respond to change?

5. What was the life goal of John the Baptist? What was the life goal of men like Andrew and Philip? What is your life goal?

Between the Lines: Truth Points

Disciple (v. 35)—both the Greeks and Jews of Jesus' day had a concept of a disciple as one who would study, adhere to, and pass along the teachings of a teacher/rabbi.

Lamb of God (v. 36)—this name of Christ identifies Jesus as the Passover Lamb without spot or blemish (Exodus 12:5), and also as the sacrificial Lamb described in Isaiah 53.

Messiah, Christ (v. 41)—"Messiah" is a transliteration (a word created for a language that is based on the way the word sounds in another language) of the Hebrew word that means "anointed" or "anointed one", which is translated as "Christos" in Greek. The Jews connected the Messiah/Christ and the Son of God together (Matthew 26:63–64, Luke 22:67–70).

Simon (v. 42)—Greek name meaning "flat-nosed." The Hebrew variation of the name, Simeon, can be translated as "hearing."

Cephas (v. 42)—an Aramaic word which is translated "Peter" in the Greek, meaning "rock."

King of Israel (v. 49)—the Jews were looking for a king to descend from David's throne; at one point in Jesus' ministry, they tried to make Jesus their king (John 6:15). Jesus is indeed the King (John 18:33–37).

Angels of God ascending and descending (v. 51)—Jesus may have been referring to Jacob's dream in Genesis 28:12–15; Jesus called Nathanael an Israelite "in whom there is no deceit" (v. 47), which also may have been a reference to Jacob, the one who deceived his father Isaac (Gen. 27).

Son of Man (v. 51)—Jesus was fond of calling Himself the Son of Man; this title of Jesus was used 83 times in the Gospels. Daniel 7:13–14 gives a powerful description of the Son of Man that clearly indicates that He is the King of kings.

> *[Evangelism] is a matter, not merely of informing, but also of inviting.*
>
> J. I. PACKER

LIFE LESSON 31

PREACHING GOD'S MESSAGE

- **Red Line Verse:** *"Blessed are the pure in heart, for they shall see God."* (Matthew 5:8)

- **Red Line Statement:** Jesus taught us how to experience God's blessings by exercising the godly character God instills in followers of Christ.

- **Red Line Connection:** Only through Christ are we able to fulfill His great teachings.

- **Focal Passage:** Matthew 5:1–12

 Listen Attentively to the Lesson

1. Tell the story of Matthew 5:1–12 in your own words.

   Context: Jesus' popularity was increasing rapidly. He traveled throughout Galilee teaching, preaching, and healing, and His fame spread throughout all Syria. People brought their sick and demon-possessed to Jesus, and He healed them. His following had now grown to become a multitude (4:23–25). The Sermon on the Mount took place when Jesus pulled away from the masses to teach His followers (5:1), thus we can be sure that these teachings apply directly to the life of the believer, the disciple of Christ. Jesus sat down in the disciples' midst, which was a position of power and authority; in this day, the king sat while others stood. We typically call these 12 verses the Beatitudes because of the repetition of the world "blessed" (*beatus* in Latin). To choose to live by Christ's teachings truly is a blessing.

2. Reconstruct Matthew 5:1–12 together, including as many details as your small group remembers.

3. Read the passage aloud together from Scripture, confirming the facts of the story. Amend any details suggested by small-group members that did not accurately represent the Scripture.

Investigate the Facts of the Lesson

Use these questions to guide small-group members to investigate the facts of this passage.

1. Who was Jesus addressing in this teaching (v. 1)?

   Jesus was talking to His disciples. In Luke's account, Luke mentions a "crowd of His disciples" that were among the great masses (Luke 6:17), indicating that Jesus was likely speaking to more than His inner group of 12. It is significant to note that Jesus was not teaching to the general masses; those who are without Christ cannot fulfill Christ's teachings in the Beatitudes. We must have the help of the Holy Spirit.

2. Do you see connections between the Beatitudes and the Ten Commandments?

   Possible answer: Both passages teach us how to live in relationship with God and others.

3. What is the word that Jesus repeated several times to introduce each point He was making?

   Jesus repeated "blessed." Jesus' words of blessings likely brought refreshment to the disciples who originally heard this teaching because they were living under the Law. You may want to briefly note Deuteronomy 27:15–26, where Moses repeated the word "cursed" several times. Although the Law did also provide blessings for those who kept it, Jesus fulfilled the demands of the Law by His sacrifice and replaced the "curses" with "blessings."

4. What other details do you see in this passage?

Allow your small group to share other details that stand out to them and discuss the significance of each point.

 Find the purpose of the lesson
Use these questions to guide small-group members to discover God's purpose for the passage.

1. What does it mean to be poor in spirit (v. 3)? What is the opposite of being poor in spirit?

We're poor in spirit when we recognize that we're spiritually bankrupt apart from Christ. When we understand that we have a great sin debt that we cannot pay on our own, we realize our total dependence upon Jesus, we give our lives to Him, and we inherit the kingdom—we're blessed! The opposite of being poor in spirit is to think too highly of our own merit. Jesus isn't teaching us to see ourselves as worthless; we're a precious treasure to Him (Malachi 3:17). However, our righteousness amounts only to filthy rags (Isaiah 64:6).

2. In verse 4, Jesus is offering a blessing to those who are experiencing brokenness.

a. When we as Christians become broken over our sin, how is it that God brings us comfort?

Possible answer: We're comforted to know that Jesus paid the penalty for our sins on the Cross; He is faithful to forgive us and cleanse us when we confess our sins (1 John 1:9).

b. Why should we be broken over our sin? Why should our sin bother us?

As your small group responds, you could point them to the Garden of Eden and how sin interferes with our relationship with God, or you could point them to the Cross where Christ paid the ultimate price as payment for our sins.

c. How do you balance the need to be broken over your sin with the need to accept God's forgiveness to move forward in your life? Is guilt God's plan for you?

The Holy Spirit convicts us of our sins, but after we repent of those sins and receive God's forgiveness, any lingering guilt is not from God. He wants us to receive the comfort He gives. Because of Christ, we are to walk in victory, not guilt and shame.

3. In verse 5, Jesus commended meekness and offered a great promise to the gentle.

a. Biblical meekness is characterized by one who controls his or her strength. Why does meekness require such a great measure of personal character? Of faith?

Possible answers: Meekness requires putting our fleshly responses under the authority of Christ. We do not act upon our emotions, and we trust God to be the righteous Judge. We yield to His authority to right the wrongs we may suffer.

b. How was Jesus the ultimate display of meekness? How does the meekness of Christians bear witness of the power of Christ to those who are not yet saved?

Jesus exercised great restraint throughout His ministry. "When He was reviled, [He] did not revile in return; when He suffered, He did not threaten, but committed Himself to Him who judges righteously" (1 Peter 2:23 NKJV). When we follow Jesus' example and choose to be meek instead of retaliating or seeking after our own interests, we allow the unsaved to see that Christ can give us an inner strength to glorify Him in every situation. God can use us to display the mercy and grace He has extended to mankind as He patiently draws sinners unto Himself.

4. In verse 6, Jesus addresses what we crave, what motivates us—what we seek for ourselves. Are you currently getting stronger or weaker in your longing for God's righteousness in your life, and why? Is there anything you are doing that affects your focus on God's righteousness?

    Encourage everyone to consider how lifestyle choices, habits, hobbies, ministry, worship, or other experiences can enhance or inhibit a deep longing for the righteousness of God.

5. How do Christ's teachings in Matthew 6:14–15 and Luke 6:31 reinforce what Jesus taught in verse 7?

    Matthew 6:14–15 is Jesus' teaching on our need to forgive others, just as we seek God's forgiveness. Luke 6:31 is what we often call the Golden Rule. We are called to extend mercy to others, just as we need God to be merciful to us. We are grateful that God doesn't give us the punishment we deserve.

6. Consider verse 9. Do you tend to be a peacemaker or a troublemaker? How is your choice of friends affecting your ability and desire to be a peacemaker?

    Allow your small group to respond. Verse 9 is a powerful encouragement to be people who bring peace, not strife or chaos; God's children are to be known as peacemakers.

7. For the persecuted Christian, why would a promise of the kingdom of heaven stir up hope?

    This world's troubles are temporary. The persecuted can look forward to a final reward of a peaceful home in the presence of God for all of eternity.

8. Which word or phrase stands out to you from verse 11?

Discuss your experiences of possible persecution or revilement. Note the important word falsely. *May our actions never give cause for others to speak poorly of Christianity.*

9. What other truths from this passage stand out to you? What else can we learn about God or learn about being a follower of Christ?

Allow everyone to respond. Share any other points of spiritual growth that the Holy Spirit brings to your attention.

Experience the Truth of the Lesson

Use these questions to guide small-group members to allow God's transformational truths to reshape their hearts and minds.

1. Jesus taught that true righteousness and godly character flow from within our hearts, while the Pharisees of Jesus' day were teaching that righteousness was made up of outward actions, such as praying, tithing, fasting, and obeying rules. Jesus said in Matthew 5:20, "For I say to you that unless your righteousness surpasses that of the scribes and Pharisees, you will not enter the kingdom of heaven." Was there a time in your life when you were counting on your outward actions to bring you righteousness? What caused the change in your life when you realized that righteousness could only flow from what Jesus has done within your heart?

After your small group members have shared their personal experiences, ask them how they might help someone who is trapped in a pharisaical attitude—counting on their good works for salvation.

2. Look again at verse 8. None of us are pure on our own. Without Christ, we would have no hope of seeing God. The Greek in

verse 8 indicates one who is pure because he or she has been purified, cleansed, or made pure. Take a moment to reflect on what Jesus has done for you, making you pure, so that you can indeed have the privilege of seeing God.

Allow your small group to respond.

3. Which of the Beatitudes is nearest to your heart today? Why?

Allow your small group to respond.

Between the Lines: Truth Points

Poor (v. 3)—from a Greek word meaning "to crouch."

Gentle (v. 5)—meek, humble.

Righteousness (v. 6)—being right with God; also often translated as justice.

Mercy (v. 7)—a compassion of thought and action that causes one not to invoke the punishment that a guilty party deserves.

Pure (v. 8)—unsoiled, uncontaminated, unalloyed.

Reward (v. 12)—*wages;* a word also used to mean payment for services.

> *Jesus had a forgiving and understanding heart. If He lives within us, mercy will temper our relationships with our fellow men.*
> BILLY GRAHAM

LIFE LESSON 32

DISPLAYING GOD'S POWER

Red Line Verse: *Those who were in the boat worshiped Him, saying, "You are certainly God's Son!"* (Matthew 14:33)

Red Line Statement: Jesus performed many miracles that displayed His power and authority as the Son of God.

Red Line Connection: Jesus revealed Himself as the Messiah and Son of God so that mankind might follow Him and be saved.

Focal Passage: Matthew 14:22–33

 Listen Attentively to the Lesson

1. Tell the story of Matthew 14:22–33 in your own words.

   Context: When Jesus miraculously fed the 5,000, His disciples didn't fully comprehend what Jesus had accomplished (Mark 6:52). However, the crowd was so greatly impacted by His power that they were about to take Jesus by force to make Him their king (John 6:15). Jesus told His disciples to get into the boat and head toward Bethsaida (Mark 6:45), while Jesus dealt with the crowd to send them away. It was on this same night that Jesus would give another great display of His deity to the disciples by walking on water.

2. Reconstruct Matthew 14:22–33 together, including as many details as your small group remembers.

3. Read the passage aloud together from Scripture, confirming the facts of the story. Amend any details suggested by small-group members that did not accurately represent the Scripture.

Investigate the Facts of the Lesson
Use these questions to guide small-group members to investigate the facts of this passage.

1. After ministering to the multitudes, Jesus pulled away for prayer. What was the atmosphere Jesus chose for this extended time of prayer with His Father (v. 23)?

    Jesus chose a place of solitude. He was away from the activity and distractions of the village and completely alone.

2. What was the atmosphere like for the disciples in the boat (v. 24)? What would have been the sights, sounds, and sensations these men were experiencing?

    The wind was up and tossing the boat in the waves. Mark's account indicates the disciples were having difficulty rowing (Mark 6:48). The wind and waves were probably creating a lot of noise, and the men were in the darkness of night. Perhaps the men were experiencing anxiety, frustration, and chaos.

3. When the disciples saw the figure on the water but did not realize it was Jesus, what words did Jesus use to calm their fears (v. 27)?

> *Jesus said, "Take courage, it is I; do not be afraid" (v. 27). They must have recognized His voice because He didn't call Himself by name. As followers of Christ, it is enough to know Jesus is with us; His presence calms our fears. "It is I" could also be translated, "I AM," a name of God (Exodus 3:14).*

4. What caused Peter to sink (vv. 30–31)?

> *Peter became afraid because of the wind and began to doubt. He took His focus off the power of Christ and instead focused on the circumstances. Jesus called Peter's faith "little."*

5. Why did the disciples worship Jesus when they were finally together in the boat (v. 33)?

> *Your small group may discuss the question of what point it was that the disciples were convinced that Jesus was the Son of God. Was it when Jesus walked on water, when His power sustained Peter to walk on water, when Jesus rescued Peter, or when the wind ceased after Jesus and Peter got into the boat?*

6. What other details do you see in this passage?

> *Allow your small group to share other details that stand out to them and discuss the significance of each point.*

Find the purpose of the lesson

Use these questions to guide small-group members to discover God's purpose for the passage.

1. The disciples at first experienced needless fear because they didn't recognize it was Jesus walking on the water. When have you experienced needless fear because you did not recognize the presence of God in your situation?

Allow your small group to respond. Often we struggle when problems arise because we feel helpless, alone, or attacked, but our fears dissipate when we recognize God's presence with us.

2. Does Peter exhibit any admirable qualities in this story? Is there an example that Peter sets for us, or did he simply fail?

   Allow your small group to discuss. Certainly Peter's faith waned, but he had enough faith to get out of the boat to attempt something beyond himself. Note that Jesus didn't ask Peter to get out of the boat—Peter desired to be out on the water with Jesus! Peter's request was pleasing to Christ, and He was willing to grant Peter's desire. Note also that Peter recognized Jesus' authority (v. 28); Peter knew it was in Jesus' power to allow him, a mere man, to walk on water.

3. When Peter asked Jesus to allow him to walk on the water, Jesus gave one simple instruction: "Come" (v. 29). Peter had never walked on water before, nor had he ever seen it done, but Jesus gave no further instruction or explanation. Are you willing to obey the command, "Come," or do you try to require God to give you more details before you're willing to obey Him by faith?

   Allow your small group to respond. Encourage them to evaluate their faith as it is measured by their willingness to follow God's instructions. As we study God's inner workings with men and women in the Old and New Testaments, we witness that God does indeed expect His people to follow His leadership by faith and not sight. Without faith, it is impossible to please God (see Hebrews 11:6).

4. Jesus was very purposeful with the timing and circumstances that allowed Him to do a great work in the disciples' lives that night. How has God been purposeful in your life? What have you learned?

   Encourage your small group to appreciate the spiritual growth God has given them as He has purposefully guided them through faith-building experiences.

5. What other truths from this passage stand out to you? What else can we learn about God or learn about being a follower of Christ?

Allow everyone to respond. Share any other points of spiritual growth that the Holy Spirit brings to your attention.

Experience the Truth of the Lesson

Use these questions to guide small-group members to allow God's transformational truths to reshape their hearts and minds.

1. Peter attempted to do something beyond himself. He wanted to do something that was only possible through the power of Christ. What are you attempting to do that is only possible through Christ's power in your life?

Allow your small group to respond. If your members are unable to say they are serving the Lord in ways that are beyond their own strength, take time to discuss what God might be saying to them. How can your small group respond in faith to this lesson?

2. After rescuing Him, Jesus asked Peter, "Why did you doubt?" (v. 31) In your own life, what is the cause of those times when you doubt? What is the remedy to doubt?

Be prepared to share from your own life.

3. What does it mean to you that Jesus reached down His hand and pulled Peter out of the water?

Jesus is our Rescuer. We don't need to be afraid to step out in faith when we remember that Jesus is with us. He loves us enough to rescue us when we fall because of our weaknesses.

4. Some people live their lives much like the other disciples did that

night—they never get out of the boat. They never respond to God's greatness.

a. What is life like for those who always remain "in the boat"?

Possible answer: In the boat, there is little risk; those in the boat watch as others step out in faith. However, in the boat, there are limitations to how we might bring glory to God and display His power in our lives.

b. Do you want to be a part of a church that stays in the boat, or do you want to be part of a church that joins Jesus out in deep waters?

Encourage your small group to stay positive about the possibilities God affords a church that operates in faith, rather than talking down churches who may be struggling in their faith. Remind everyone that a church that walks by faith is made up of a body of believers who are individually willing to walk by faith. What joy is stirred up when we talk about going deeper with Christ! His power is limitless, which means that our ability to be used by God to do great things is limitless.

c. How will you respond to God's greatness? Are you in or out of the boat?

Encourage every person to respond to God's invitation to "get out of the boat" to magnify the glory of the Lord.

Between the Lines: Truth Points

Fourth watch of the night (v. 25)—One division of time used in this era was the watch, based on increments of time for soldiers or watchmen to be on duty. The fourth watch of the night would have been 3:00–6:00 a.m.

Ghost (v. 26)—the Greek word *phantasma*, also translated "apparition" or "phantom."

> *Twenty years from now, you will be more disappointed by the risks you didn't take than by the ones you did. Defeat tomorrow's regret by moving forward and getting into the faith zone today.*
> JOHN C. MAXWELL

LIFE LESSON 33

JESUS SHOWS CARE AND CONCERN

● **Red Line Verse:** *And He said to her, "Daughter, your faith has made you well; go in peace."* (Luke 8:48)

● **Red Line Statement:** Jesus showed compassion for the suffering by healing the sick and raising the dead. He displayed His authority over death and His life-giving power.

● **Red Line Connection:** The Son of God has power to give us hope, healing, and life.

● **Focal Passage:** Luke 8:40–56

 Listen Attentively to the Lesson

1. Tell the story of Luke 8:40–56 in your own words.

   Context: After healing a demoniac in the country of the Gerasenes (Luke 8:26–39, called Gadarenes in Matthew 8:28), Jesus sailed across the Sea of Galilee back to Capernaum, an important city in the ministry of Jesus and the place described as "his own city" (Matthew 9:1). By now, Jesus' ministry was well underway, and His fame continued to grow through His teaching, preaching, and healing. Luke 8:41–56 weaves together two stories of people whose lives were forever changed by the compassion and power of Jesus Christ. The woman with the issue of blood didn't appear to have any personal connection with

Jairus, but these two individuals were thrown together in time and circumstance as they came face to face with the Son of God on a particular day on the streets of Capernaum.

2. Reconstruct Luke 8:40–56 together, including as many details as your small group remembers.

3. Read the passage aloud together from Scripture, confirming the facts of the story. Amend any details suggested by small-group members that did not accurately represent the Scripture.

Investigate the Facts of the Lesson

Use these questions to guide small-group members to investigate the facts of this passage.

1. Who are the people involved in this passage, and how do the stories of Jairus and the woman with the issue of blood intertwine?

    Those involved are Jairus, Jairus's daughter, Jairus's wife, the messenger who came from Jairus's home, the woman with the issue of blood, Jesus, the disciples (Matthew 9:19 records the disciples being in this scene; Peter, James, and John are specifically mentioned in Luke's account), the multitudes, and the mourners at Jairus's home. The stories of Jairus and the woman with the blood disorder intersect by the timing and location of their interactions with Jesus. Note the great contrast between the woman and Jairus. The woman was an outcast and was out of money, but Jairus had position and resources. The woman had suffered 12 years, while the man had enjoyed 12 years with his daughter. Both fell at Jesus' feet at their point of need.

2. Why did the woman's covert act of touching Jesus' garment become exposed to the multitudes? Why would her testimony be powerful to the Jews in the multitude?

Jesus felt the power of healing go out from Him, and He wanted the person who received that power to be revealed. Jesus allowed this woman the opportunity to bear witness to what Jesus Christ had done for her. She had dealt with an illness that not only affected her physically, but also socially and spiritually. Because of her issue of blood, she would have been considered unclean, as well as anything she sat upon and anyone who came in physical contact with her or the place where she rested (Leviticus. 15:19–25). For 12 years she had been an outcast (Numbers 5:2), but this "untouchable" woman was now made whole because she touched the Great Physician.

3. How did the woman's healing seemingly interfere with the healing of Jairus's daughter? What might have been going on in Jairus's mind when Jesus stopped along the road to talk with the woman with the issue of blood?

   While Jesus was speaking with the healed woman, someone came from Jairus's home to announce the daughter's death. Discuss the emotions Jairus may have experienced while he waited for Jesus to go to his home to heal his daughter. If they were in Jairus's place, would your small-group members have been able to rejoice for the woman who was healed, or would they have felt frustrated at this delay?

4. What other details do you see in this passage?

   Allow your small group to share other details that stand out to them and discuss the significance of each point.

Find the purpose of the lesson
   Use these questions to guide small-group members to discover God's purpose for the passage.

1. Jesus was becoming well known in the region where He ministered.

a. What kind of reputation did Jesus have among the people that would cause the multitudes to be waiting on his return (v. 40), and cause Jairus and the woman to seek Jesus' help?

Possible answer: Jesus had a reputation as One sent from God who possessed great powers and a compassion to help others.

b. Why did people believe these things about Jesus?

Many people had heard Jesus teach and preach and had been eyewitnesses of His miracles of healing the sick and demon-possessed. Word also spread because these eyewitnesses and the people He had made well were sharing the good news about Jesus.

c. Today, what kind of reputation do people in this nation attribute to Jesus?

Possible answer: Those who have had a personal encounter with Jesus Christ know and believe in His name. Some unbelievers may have a positive opinion of Jesus based on the testimonies of Christians, but many people dismiss Christ as a good man, a prophet, or a myth. They do not see any value in knowing Jesus personally.

d. Why do people believe these things about Jesus? How are you affecting the thinking of others as they form their opinions about who Jesus is?

Jesus continues to display His power, healing people and giving them victory over death. Are we spreading His fame? Are we telling others about the great things Jesus does every day? The evil one spreads lies about the name of Christ, but we can overcome those lies with the truth about Jesus the Savior. We must speak His name.

2. Before the woman met Jesus, she had spent all she had trying to get healed (v. 43).

a. What are some of the ways people try to "purchase" healing for their souls?

The prosperity gospel—expecting God to do something for those who give money; trying to purchase salvation with good works; New Age ideas of healing with crystals, stones, and therapy; those who believe that psycho-babble can heal the hunger of their souls.

b. What would you say to someone who has tried other means to solve their problems to convince them to come to Jesus for help and healing?

Allow your small group to respond.

3. From the reaction of Peter in verse 45, many people were in physical contact with Jesus, but only one woman reached out to touch Him in faith. Place yourself in the crowd that day and think about the way you daily operate in your relationship with Jesus. Are you traveling along life's road with a crowd of Christians, experiencing casual contact with Jesus, or are you the one who is reaching out to have personal contact with Jesus?

We will fall short in our faith and miss out on experiencing God's power if we do not reach out for Jesus. We need His personal touch in our lives every day.

4. While Jesus was talking with the woman, Jairus's daughter died. Jairus's circumstances appeared to have worsened while he was forced to wait on Jesus to accomplish something in someone else's life. Do you ever struggle to be patient for God to come to your rescue? Have you ever sensed that perhaps God was allowing you to endure a struggle because He was working in someone else's life? Were you willing to endure so that others might be saved?

As your small group responds, encourage everyone to realize that it's not that God can only help one person at a time; sometimes God chooses to display

His glory through a Christian's struggles in order to bring others to Christ. We often assume that our trials are all about us, when sometimes God is working in others' lives through us.

5. When Jesus arrived at Jairus's home, whom did He allow to enter (v. 51)? While Jesus had publically performed many miracles, why would this miracle be performed privately?

   Only the parents and Peter, James, and John were allowed to enter. We can only speculate about Jesus' reasoning. However, we can note that Jesus performed miracles out of love and compassion for the hurting, and not simply to show off His powers to the masses. In this case, the scoffing unbelievers were left outside, and the parents were able to experience this precious miracle with privacy.

68

6. What other truths from this passage stand out to you? What else can we learn about God or learn about being a follower of Christ?

   Allow everyone to respond. Share any other points of spiritual growth that the Holy Spirit brings to your attention.

Experience the Truth of the Lesson

Use these questions to guide small-group members to allow God's transformational truths to reshape their hearts and minds.

1. Many ridiculed Jesus for attempting to "wake up" the deceased little girl (v. 53). Why have you chosen to place your faith in Jesus Christ to one day raise you from the dead?

   Share Ephesians 2:1. As Christians, we have already passed from death unto life!

2. In this passage of Scripture, how does Jesus Christ connect His power with our faith?

Jesus told the woman her faith had made her well (v. 48), and He instructed Jairus to believe and his daughter would be made well (v. 50). It was Jesus' power that brought healing to the woman and raised Jairus's daughter from the dead, and because of what Jesus said to them, we are encouraged to realize the importance of faith.

3. In your practical faith—the faith in which you daily operate—how much power and authority have you ascribed to Jesus? How will studying this passage influence your practical faith?

    Allow your small group to respond.

Between the Lines: Truth Points

Official of the synagogue (v. 41)—also called the ruler of the synagogue, this individual cared for the facility and selected participants to perform such duties as pray and read Scriptures during the Sabbath services.

Hemorrhage (v. 43)—translated "issue of blood" in the KJV, a condition of heavy, uncontrollable bleeding.

Touched the fringe of His cloak (v. 44)—Luke 6:19 records that people were being healed by touching Jesus; if the woman had heard these reports, it explains why she would believe that touching His garment could bring healing to her.

Asleep (v. 52)—Jesus was not confused about the status of the little girl. In John 11:11–14, Jesus used the same metaphor of sleep to describe death, but He also clearly stated that Lazarus was dead (v. 14). Jesus' description of death as mere sleep shows His power, that raising the dead is no more difficult than awakening someone from sleep. The Epistles also contain several instances of this metaphor of sleep (see 1 Thessalonians 4:13–15).

> *A prayerful heart and an obedient heart will learn, very slowly*
> *and not without sorrow, to stake everything on God Himself.*
>
> ELISABETH ELLIOT

LIFE LESSON 34

Jesus Is Messiah

● **Red Line Verse:** *"You are the Christ, the Son of the Living God."* (Matthew 16:16)

● **Red Line Statement:** Knowing the time was approaching for Him to suffer and die on the Cross, Jesus prepared His disciples to stand firmly on the truth that He was the Christ.

● **Red Line Connection:** Jesus knew He was the Christ and wanted others to know.

● **Focal Passage:** Matthew 16:13–20

 Listen Attentively to the Lesson

1. Tell the story of Matthew 16:13–20 in your own words.

   Context: While Jesus was well known as a healer, teacher, and preacher, there was some confusion among people about just exactly who Jesus was. The disciples had already professed Jesus as the Christ on other occasions (John 1:41, 49; 6:68–69; Matthew 14:33), but the discussion recorded in Matthew 16:13–20 was different. In this discussion, Jesus solidified in their minds some truths about His identity as preparation for His disciples to then hear that as Christ, Jesus would be crucified and rise again.

2. Reconstruct Matthew 16:13–20 together, including as many details as your small group remembers.

3. Read the passage aloud together from Scripture, confirming the facts of the story. Amend any details suggested by small-group members that did not accurately represent the Scripture.

Investigate the Facts of the Lesson

Use these questions to guide small-group members to investigate the facts of this passage.

1. Jesus already knew what was in the hearts of men; He only asked questions for the benefit of others. What were the two questions that Jesus asked His disciples (v. 13, 15), and what value was it for the disciples to answer these questions?

    Jesus asked the disciples to tell Him what others were saying about His identity, and then to tell Him whom they believed that He was. Jesus wasn't being egotistical in asking these questions, nor was He evaluating the success of His campaign to draw people into faith in Him. These questions were for the benefit of the disciples, allowing them to thoroughly think through all they had seen and heard and then affirm who Jesus was.

2. Who were people suggesting that Jesus really was (v. 14)?

    John the Baptist and Jesus were seen together at Jesus' baptism. John the Baptist by now had already been beheaded by Herod (14:10), but perhaps people hadn't seen Jesus and John together nor had they heard of John the Baptist's death. Perhaps Elijah was suggested because of the promise of Malachi 4:5: "Behold, I am going to send you Elijah the prophet before the coming of the great and terrible day of the LORD." Jeremiah "the weeping prophet" was another name suggested. These suggestions indicate how little the general public understood about who Jesus was, but also shows that Jesus had created a stir among the Jews and people recognized Him as sent from God.

3. According to Jesus, how did Peter come to realize that Jesus was the Son of God (v. 17)?

Jesus said that it wasn't by human persuasion but by God's revelation that Peter recognized His identity as Christ.

4. What other details do you see in this passage?

Allow your small group to share other details that stand out to them and discuss the significance of each point.

Find the purpose of the lesson

Use these questions to guide small-group members to discover God's purpose for the passage.

73

1. Compare what Jesus said in verse 17 to Paul's words in 1 Corinthians 2:1–5. How do these truths shape your thoughts about telling others about Jesus? What is God's role in convincing people of the truth of who Jesus is?

Possible answer: Even the most polished gospel presentation cannot convince a person to believe in Jesus Christ; this persuasion is a work of God as the Holy Spirit draws men. However, God uses our words of witness in His process of convincing men of the truth. Paul was glad to share the truth of Christ despite his fear, demonstrating the power of God and the work of the Holy Spirit. This same humble attitude can be in us as we witness to others.

2. Think about what Jesus proclaimed to Peter about the foundation of the church (v. 18).

a. When did Jesus first call Peter a rock?

Jesus called him Cephas (the Aramaic word for "stone") when He first called him to be a disciple (John 1:42).

b. According to 1 Corinthians 3:11, who is the foundation of our faith?

Jesus, not Peter, is the foundation of our faith, and thus the foundation of the church. Peter himself understood this, and he testified of Christ being the fulfillment of Old Testament prophecies pointing to Jesus as the Chief Cornerstone (Acts 4:11; 1 Peter 2:6—8). What is the rock that the Church is built upon? Peter said it: Jesus is the Christ, the Son of the Living God. This is our foundational truth. And building upon this foundation, God uses us just as He used Peter to be "living stones" for Him (1 Peter 2:4—5).

c. Since Jesus is the foundation of our church, how does this truth shape the way we "do" church? What is our purpose? What is our focus? What is our motivation for connecting with one another as believers?

As your small group discusses the purpose, focus, and motivation of the church, Jesus is the answer to who we are and why we're unified as a body of believers.

3. Jesus proclaimed that the gates of Hades would not prevail over His church (v. 18). This assurance of Christ is meaningful to us as Christians on many levels.

a. How would you imagine these words of Christ encourage our brothers and sisters in Christ who are persecuted for their faith?

Possible answer: Their suffering is not in vain. Though evil regimes may try to extinguish the name of Christ, men who do evil deeds will never be able to obliterate Jesus Christ and His followers.

b. How do Christ's words bring assurance to your life?

Possible answer: Because of the evil, injustice, and suffering we see in the world, we may feel tempted to believe that darkness is overtaking the light. However, we know and believe that Jesus Christ is triumphant and His church will prevail.

c. How does a church display her faith that the powers of evil will not overtake us?

Discuss actions of faith within a church body. We do not operate in fear; even in the face of challenges, we operate in faith because of the promise of Jesus.

4. Jesus told Peter He would give him the keys to the kingdom of heaven (v. 19), and Peter was indeed one of the great evangelists of the early church. As a Christian, you also hold the keys that unlock the "mystery"—you know what is necessary for a person to enter heaven. Jesus is the only way to heaven, and we are keepers of the truth. Think about this analogy that Jesus has given to us: we hold the keys to heaven. How do you react to this responsibility?

    Allow your small group to respond. Talk about the sacrifices that go along with having this great privilege and responsibility of having the "keys" to salvation. Who needs us to share with them? Those who live close, those who live far away, those who want to hear, those who don't show any interest in the gospel…what is our calling?

5. The idea of binding and loosing that Jesus talked about in verse 19 was a common expression to the Jews, and it expressed the idea of forbidding and permitting. Jesus repeated this statement in Matthew 18:18 as He spoke to the disciples. The disciples were leaders in the early church and God used them to form our doctrine, teaching us what is forbidden and permitted as we live for Christ. How would you respond to people who say that the Bible's teachings, particularly teachings on what is forbidden

and permitted, are outdated and do not apply in today's culture?

Allow your small group to share their thoughts, and encourage a strong stance from your small group to hold to the authority of Scripture throughout all generations. God's truths do not change.

6. What other truths from this passage stand out to you? What else can we learn about God or learn about being a follower of Christ?

    Allow everyone to respond. Share any other points of spiritual growth that the Holy Spirit brings to your attention.

Experience the Truth of the Lesson

Use these questions to guide small-group members to allow God's transformational truths to reshape their hearts and minds.

1. Think through the questions Jesus posed to the disciples.

    a. Who do people say that Jesus is?

    Many in the world say that Jesus was a good man, a prophet, a healer, a philosopher, a controversial figure in history, an imposter, one of many ways to God, etc.

    b. Who do people in our church say that Jesus is? What about your family? What about you?

    Allow everyone to respond.

    c. How do your thoughts and actions reflect your beliefs about who Jesus is?

    Allow everyone to respond.

2. In verse 18, Jesus is the first One to use the word *church* in the New Testament. Jesus Christ is the One who established the

church. What is the one truth about the church that you want to take away from this lesson?

Be prepared to share your own response.

3. After Jesus prepared and encouraged the disciples through this discussion, He then told them about His coming death and resurrection (vv. 21–23). How can the truths of today's focal passage give you courage to face any challenges in the future?

Allow members to share how Jesus' identity as Christ and His promises encourage them.

Between the Lines: Truth Points

Caesarea Philippi (v. 13)—a lush region of Palestine in the upper Jordan Valley. Caesarea Philippi was a site of religious activity for centuries, including pagan worship. About 40–50 years after Jesus spoke to the disciples in Caesarea Philippi, the Roman general Titus held gladiator events there, during which many Jews were put to death.

Son of Man (v. 13)—Jesus frequently referred to Himself with this term that reflects His humanity.

Christ (v. 16)—from the Greek word *Christos*, meaning "anointed." The word corresponds to the Hebrew word translated "Messiah."

Peter/rock (v. 18)—Jesus said, "You are Peter [*petros*—a stone], and on this rock [*petra*—a large rock] I will build My church." Collectively, Christians throughout time have been living stones built upon the cornerstone of Jesus Christ as He builds His church.

Church (v. 18)—The Greek word *ekklesia* was a common term used in a secular sense in Jesus' day; an *ekklesia*, literally a "called-out assembly," was the term used for an assembly of Greek citizens who helped to govern a city or district. Jesus remade the word as the first One to use the word in the New Testament, designating His body of believers as a called-out assembly.

Gates of Hades (v. 18)—For the Jews, the gates of a city were where people in authority made decisions and conducted business; the gates of Hades may be said to represent the limited power of death and Satan.

A true faith in Jesus Christ will not suffer us to be idle. No, it is an active, lively, restless principle; it fills the heart, so that it cannot be easy till it is doing something for Jesus Christ.

GEORGE WHITEFIELD

IT IS FINISHED

It was the grand finale. When Jesus uttered "It is finished" while hanging on those rugged crossbeams, the "it" of that phrase encompassed more than what appeared to be happening on that Friday. Yes, the agony that He suffered for our sins was complete, and so too was His earthly ministry. But the "it" that was finished when Jesus breathed His last was more than that; it was the culmination of a story of redemption that God had been writing since Adam and Eve ate the wrong fruit. The *thin red line* was by the time of Christ centuries long. It led to a pool of divine blood at the foot of the Cross, but *it* was mission complete. We tie a beautiful red bow on that moment of time on the thin red line, and we follow the trail of crimson that leads to our heavenly home.

LIFE LESSON 35

THE KING HAS COME

Red Line Verse: *The crowds going ahead of Him, and those who followed, were shouting, "Hosanna to the Son of David; Blessed is He who comes in the name of the LORD; Hosanna in the highest!"* (Matthew 21:9)

Red Line Statement: Jesus made His identity as King of kings and Messiah known when He entered into Jerusalem mounted on a colt, receiving the praise of the Jews.

Red Line Connection: Jesus is the One and only rightful heir to the throne of David. He is the fulfillment of God's promises to the Jews as King of kings.

Focal Passage: Matthew 21:1–11

 Listen Attentively to the Lesson

1. Tell the story of Matthew 21:1–11 in your own words.

   Context: Up to this point in Jesus' ministry, Jesus spent much of His time outside of Jerusalem. Jesus knew the corrupt Jewish leaders of Jerusalem would one day be instrumental in His crucifixion, so He avoided unnecessary confrontations in order to obey His Heavenly Father's perfect will for the timing of His death on the Cross. In fact, Jesus often instructed people not to tell about His miracles or to reveal His identity as Messiah, honoring His Father's timing. When the time of His crucifixion was finally drawing near, Jesus was willing to walk into the will of His Father as tensions mounted in Jerusalem. Luke spoke of Jesus' resolve in this way: "Now it came to pass, when the time had come for Him to be received up, that He steadfastly set His face to go to Jerusalem" (Luke 9:51 NKJV).

   In Jerusalem, Jesus claimed to be one with the Father. The Jews tried to seize Jesus and stone Him, but He escaped (John 10:22–39). The pressure was building. Soon after, Jesus' friend Lazarus became sick and the sisters Mary and Martha sent for Jesus to come to them in Bethany, just two miles outside of Jerusalem. His disciples tried to stop Jesus from risking the danger in Jerusalem (John 11:8), but Jesus knew that His raising of Lazarus from the dead would be an important stepping stone to bring many to faith in Him. Jesus also knew this miracle would create more uproar in Jerusalem, which would contribute to the hostile feelings of the Jewish leaders and fuel their anger toward Him.

   This Life Lesson explores the events of the Sunday before Jesus' crucifixion. Not only is Jesus' triumphal entry significant because Jesus orchestrated a public demonstration of His identity as Messiah, but this event was also one of the final blows that angered the chief priests and scribes enough to plot the death of Jesus.

2. Reconstruct Matthew 21:1–11 together, including as many details as your small group remembers.

3. Read the passage aloud together from Scripture, confirming the facts of the story. Amend any details suggested by small-group members that did not accurately represent the Scripture.

 Investigate the Facts of the Lesson
Use these questions to guide small-group members to investigate the facts of this passage.

1. What was unusual about the instructions Jesus gave the disciples (vv. 2–3)?

   The disciples didn't know who the owner of the donkey and colt was, nor how the owner would know to release the animals to them.

2. What did the people do when Jesus entered Jerusalem, and what did they say (vv. 8–9)?

   They spread their clothes on the road, along with palm branches (see John 12:13). They cried out, "Hosanna!" which is translated, "Save [us], we pray." Their proclamation came from Psalm 118:26, indicating they were elevating Jesus as King of Israel.

3. This was the week of Passover. Why is the timing of Jesus' triumphal entry significant?

Because it was Passover week, large crowds had gathered to Jerusalem, perhaps as many as hundreds of thousands. The people poured out praise on Jesus, which greatly angered the Pharisees and made them feel that they must do more to stop Jesus. They said to one another, "You see that you are not doing any good; look, the world has gone after Him" (John 12:19). Point out to your small group that not only was the timing important because of the crowds, but also because Jesus is our Passover Lamb.

4. What other details do you see in this passage?

Allow your small group to share other details that stand out to them and discuss the significance of each point.

 Find the purpose of the lesson

Use these questions to guide small-group members to discover God's purpose for the passage.

1. Jesus was very intentional about the way He entered into Jerusalem.

   a. How was Jesus fulfilling prophecy?

   Jesus was fulfilling Zechariah 9:9 by coming as King on the back of the foal of a donkey. Kings often paraded into a city on a majestic horse, but Jesus came on the lowly donkey, revealing His humble nature.

   b. Jesus was always very intentional about when and to whom He revealed His identity, often telling people not to tell others about His miracles. By orchestrating a plan to enter Jerusalem in this manner, what was Jesus publically declaring to the Jews?

   Jesus was declaring Himself to be the Son of David, the King of Israel, the Promised One. In John's account, the crowds called Him the King of Israel (John 12:13).

c. Though Jesus had the support of the masses, He didn't give a speech, issue a rally cry, or try to challenge the Roman government's authority. Why didn't Jesus seize the moment to be crowned King of the Jews?

Later that week, Jesus would tell Pilate, "My kingdom is not of this world" (John 18:36). Jesus is the King who reigns in man's heart, not from a political throne.

2. Think about the dramatic differences in public opinion demonstrated over the course of five days. A great multitude of people in Jerusalem offered Jesus praise and accolades on Sunday, almost like a pledge of their allegiance to Him as King. Four days later, a large group came at night to seize Him with swords and clubs in the garden of Gethsemane (Matthew 26:55). The very next day a crowd, urged on by the chief priests, cried out, "Crucify Him! Crucify Him!" (Luke 23:21; Matthew 27:20).

a. Why do you think that many eventually rejected Jesus as their King?

Possible answers: Jesus didn't come to conquer human oppressors and set them free from Roman rule, but to conquer death and sin. Jesus didn't appeal to their fleshly desires for a mighty leader. Jesus didn't have the approval of the religious leaders of the day; He challenged the status quo.

b. What does this dramatic and swift change in the public opinion of the "multitudes" reveal about mankind?

Possible answer: In our flesh, we are flawed, short-sighted, and fickle. We fall short of the glory of God (Romans 3:23). We are capable of being selfish even in our approach to God.

c. Jesus knew the cries of "Hosanna!" would soon be replaced with cries of "crucify Him!" yet He made no attempt to retain His popularity during His triumphal entry. What do Jesus' actions reveal about Him?

Possible answer: Jesus was focused on His role as Redeemer. He was determined to fulfill what His Father had sent Him to do. Obedience was more important than man's praise.

3. What other truths from this passage stand out to you? What else can we learn about God or learn about being a follower of Christ?

Allow everyone to respond. Share any other points of spiritual growth that the Holy Spirit brings to your attention.

Experience the Truth of the Lesson

Use these questions to guide small-group members to allow God's transformational truths to reshape their hearts and minds.

1. The multitudes created such a stir in Jerusalem that people asked, "Who is this?" (v. 10).

   a. How can God use the multitudes of people who make up our church to create a stir about Jesus Christ in our own city?

   Encourage your small group to think about the message you express to your community; what is the message? How do people form an opinion about what you're about as a church? How can God use us to bring praise to Jesus and cause people to begin asking, "Who is this?"

   b. In Luke's account of the triumphal entry, some of the Pharisees told Jesus to rebuke the people for their actions and words of adoration and praise, but Jesus refused (Luke 19:39–40). He would not silence their praise because of pressure from the Pharisees. How does Christ's boldness encourage you? How should we as Christians respond to rising public pressure to keep silent about Jesus?

Jesus told the Pharisees that if the people were silent, the rocks would cry out (Luke 19:40)! Discuss with your small group the pressure they may feel to be silent about Jesus in public settings and how Jesus' words to the Pharisees apply today.

2. John recorded this commentary to describe the hearts of the people in the days between Jesus' triumphal entry on Sunday and His arrest on Wednesday night: "Though He had performed so many signs before them, yet they were not believing in Him" (John 12:37). Think about Jesus as your King. What signs has He given you to encourage you in your faith? What situation in your life is Jesus bringing to your mind, challenging you to once again believe in Him? Encourage everyone to share how God is challenging him or her to live by faith.

3. Israel was divided and conquered, living under Roman occupation. They were looking for a king to descend from the throne of David to restore them and allow them to regain their promises as descendants of Abraham. How was Jesus better than their limited expectations? How would you describe Jesus as King of your life?

Allow everyone to respond. Thank God for who Jesus is: the all-powerful, reigning King over all the earth, and also the gentle, loving, and meek Son of God who chose to ride into Jerusalem on the back of a donkey.

Between the Lines Truth Points

Bethphage (v. 1)—a small village on the Mount of Olives near Bethany, just outside of Jerusalem. The word *bethphage* means "house of unripe figs."

Donkey and the colt (v. 7)—The other gospel accounts of Jesus' triumphal entry only refer to the colt and not its mother. Matthew's account doesn't contradict the other gospels; he included a detail that the other gospel writers did not. Some of Israel's judges rode donkeys during the era of the judges, before Israel's first king (Judges 10:4; 12:14).

Branches and coats in the road (v. 8)—It was customary for branches, coats, rugs, or flowers to be strewn in the path of a conqueror or king as a sign of honor and respect. Jehu received a similar reception when he was recognized as king (2 Kings 9:13).

Hosanna (v. 9)—literally, "save [us], we pray," or "save now."

> *Jesus Christ demands more complete allegiance than any dictator who ever lived. The difference is, He has a right to it.*
>
> VANCE HAVNER

LIFE LESSON 36

FINAL MOMENTS BEFORE THE ARREST

Red Line Verse: *"For this is My blood of the covenant, which is poured out for many for forgiveness of sins."* (Matthew 26:28)

Red Line Statement: Jesus ate the Passover with His disciples and instituted communion as a remembrance of Christ's life given as a new covenant between God and mankind.

Red Line Connection: Jesus was the sacrificial Lamb of God whose body was broken and blood shed to give us a new covenant with God.

Focal Passages: Matthew 26:20–30, 36–42

Listen Attentively to the Lesson

1. Tell the story of Matthew 26:20–30, 36–42 in your own words.

Context: After Jesus' triumphal entry on Sunday, He cleansed the Temple, taught, prophesied, and healed the sick while the battle raged among the religious leaders over Jesus' identity. The chief priests and scribes were plotting to kill Him, but feared the people (Luke 22:2). Judas Iscariot, one of Jesus' 12 disciples, approached them and agreed to betray Jesus for 30 pieces of silver (Matthew 26:14–16). On Thursday evening, Jesus ate the Passover as His last meal with His disciples (26:17–19). It was the night before His crucifixion, and Jesus would teach His disciples many lessons in these final hours.

2. Reconstruct Matthew 26:20–30, 36–42 together, including as many details as your small group remembers.

3. Read the passage aloud together from Scripture, confirming the facts of the story. Amend any details suggested by small-group members that did not accurately represent the Scripture.

Investigate the Facts of the Lesson

Use these questions to guide small-group members to investigate the facts of this passage.

1. The week had already been potentially stressful for the disciples. Sunday's triumphal entry created a stir throughout Jerusalem, and the Pharisees and scribes were outraged.

   a. What was the terrible news Jesus gave the disciples during the Passover meal (v. 21)?

   One of the disciples would betray Jesus.

   b. What was the response of the disciples (v. 22)? What do their responses reveal about what may have been going on in their hearts?

   They were deeply sorrowed, and each man asked Jesus if he were the guilty one. Ask your small group to explore why the disciples would ask such a question. Were they feeling weak? Were they struggling under the pressure from the Pharisees? Were they afraid? Did each man feel he was capable of being the betrayer?

   c. Were the disciples showing spiritual maturity or immaturity by asking Jesus, "Surely not I, Lord?"

Allow your small group to respond. We can at least appreciate the disciples' great sorrow over this news that someone would betray Jesus; brokenness over sin is a mark of spiritual maturity. We can also admire their willingness to be honest and transparent with Jesus as each of them asked Jesus if he was the guilty one.

2. This last meal with the disciples was significant because they were celebrating Passover.

   a. When God instituted the celebration of the Passover in the days of Moses, what was the reason for the annual celebration (Exodus 12:27)? What were the Jews supposed to remember?

      God wanted the Jews to remember for all generations that the death angel passed over them when the firstborn of Egypt were struck during the tenth and final plague that led to the deliverance of Israel out of Egyptian bondage. They were saved from death by the blood of a sacrificial lamb.

   b. What did Jesus tell His disciples was the reason for them to partake of the bread and wine (vv. 26–28)? What did Jesus want them to remember?

      Jesus wanted them to remember His broken body and shed blood. Jesus said, "Do this in remembrance of Me" (Luke 22:19).

3. In the garden, what was the "cup" Jesus prayed about (v. 39, 42)? What was Jesus' ultimate desire that He expressed in His prayer? What does Jesus teach us about prayer?

   Above all, Jesus wanted to do the will of the Father, and He taught us to pray for God's will to be done above our own desires. Your small group may have many ideas to express the meaning of the "cup" Jesus spoke of in His prayer to the Father, because Jesus was about to suffer many things. However, emphasize the magnitude of Jesus taking the sins of the world upon Himself (2 Corinthians 5:21; 1 Peter 2:24). He experienced the full effects of sin, including the feeling of separation from the Father (Mark 15:34). The cup of God's wrath was poured out upon Jesus.

4. What other details do you see in this passage?

   Allow your small group to share other details that stand out to them and discuss the significance of each point.

Find the purpose of the lesson

Use these questions to guide small-group members to discover God's purpose for the passage.

1. What was the value for Judas to know that Jesus was aware of his betrayal? How are you challenged personally by knowing that Jesus knew Judas was the betrayer, and yet He washed Judas's feet (John 13:1–5), didn't respond to Judas in anger, and didn't try to stop Judas?

   Jesus submitted to His Father's will and displayed amazing self-control that challenges us to reconsider how we should respond to people who hurt us. Would the Lord also allow us to endure hardships with difficult people so that God can achieve a greater purpose in our lives or in their lives? Are we willing to serve others who aren't showing kindness to us?

2. Jesus spoke of His blood shed for a new covenant (v. 28). Read Hebrews 8:8–13. Why did God offer a new covenant? How is grace extended in the new covenant? What words and phrases in Hebrews 8:8–13 speak to the intimate relationship that God offers us in the new covenant?

   The Israelites didn't keep the covenant God had made with their fathers (v. 9). The new covenant is a great display of God's grace, as God promises to remember our sins no more. Our unrighteousness is met with His mercy.

3. Blood sacrifices had always been an integral part of God's requirements for the pardon of sin: "without shedding of blood, there is no remission of sins" (Hebrews 9:22 NKJV).

a. How did Jesus' sacrificial death on the Cross replace the need for animal sacrifices?

Jesus was without sin, the only perfect sacrifice as the Lamb of God. His blood alone is able to atone for the sins of all of mankind and purchase our salvation. Refer to 1 Peter 3:18.

b. Because the Jewish Christians of the early church had experienced blood sacrifices, the taking of the Lord's Supper was surely a strong visual for them to remember Jesus' sacrifice on the Cross. As someone who has never had to experience blood sacrifices, how do you personally relate to the image of the bread and wine when you partake of the Lord's Supper?

Encourage your small group to discuss the significance of the Lord's Supper and ask them if they will approach the Lord's Supper any differently after studying how this experience conveys God's message of the thin red line of redemption.

4. In the garden, Jesus told Peter, James, and John about His deep sorrow, and He asked them to "keep watch" with Him (v. 38). Instead, they fell asleep.

a. How does it affect you when you know people are praying with you about a matter?

Ask everyone to think about the prayer support they offer one another as a small group.

b. The disciples let Jesus down by falling asleep in His time of sorrow. If they had realized what was about to happen, do you think they would have taken the prayer time more seriously? What keeps us from taking prayer more seriously?

Be prepared to share how prayer has made a difference in your life. Guide an open discussion about how our prayer lives can be strengthened by realizing how vital our communication with God is.

5. What other truths from this passage stand out to you? What else can we learn about God or learn about being a follower of Christ?

Allow everyone to respond. Share any other points of spiritual growth that the Holy Spirit brings to your attention.

 Experience the Truth of the Lesson

Use these questions to guide small-group members to allow God's transformational truths to reshape their hearts and minds.

1. When Jesus instituted what we now call the Lord's Supper, He told the disciples to partake of the bread and wine; He wanted them to personally experience it by taking in the food and drink. As a Christian, how are you personally connected with Jesus' death on the Cross?

Guide your small-group members to fully embrace the sacrifice that Jesus made on the Cross to pay the penalty for their sins. Jesus redeemed us; His blood purchased our salvation. Ask them how their lives have been changed by believing that Jesus didn't choose to die just for some abstract concept of "sin in the world," but He chose to give His life on the Cross so that He might purchase our salvation.

2. The disciples didn't know what was about to happen in the garden, but Jesus did. He told Peter to "keep watching and praying that you may not enter into temptation; the spirit is willing, but the

flesh is weak" (v. 41). You also don't know your future, but God does. Read verse 41 again, allowing Jesus to give these instructions to you for today. How can a person live practically by the words of verse 41?

Challenge everyone to embrace Christ's words for a lifestyle of prayer and watchfulness.

3. Which scene from this study has gripped your attention more today—the scene around the table for the Passover meal or the events in the garden of Gethsemane? Why?

Encourage every person to share an answer.

Between the Lines: Truth Points

"Surely not I, Lord?" (v. 22)—The wording of the question in the negative suggests that each disciple expected to hear "no," yet each man asked the question rather than emphatically denying that he could be the betrayer. (Later in the evening, Peter denied that he could ever stumble in his loyalty to Jesus when Jesus made the statement in verse 31, "You will all fall away because of Me this night.") Also note that the disciples' reaction to Jesus' news that there was a betrayer among them seemed to be shock; Judas had hidden his evil intents well.

Hymn (v. 30)—Particular psalms were designated to be recited as part of the Passover celebration in homes as well as in the Temple as Passover lambs were being slain. These groupings of psalms were called "Hallel" or "Praise Thou." Scholars believe that Psalms 113 to 118 were recited in homes, thus one of these passages may have been the hymn that Jesus and the disciples sang before going to the Mount of Olives.

Gethsemane (v. 36)—means "oil press." Located on the Mount of Olives.

Two sons of Zebedee (v. 37)—James and John.

> *Joy in affliction is rooted in the hope of resurrection, but our*
> *experience of suffering also deepens the root of that hope*
>
> JOHN PIPER

LIFE LESSON 37

ACCEPTING OR REJECTING JESUS

- **Red Line Verse:** *Jesus answered, "You say correctly that I am a king. For this I have been born, and for this I have come into the world, to testify to the truth. Everyone who is of the truth hears My voice."* (John 18:37)

- **Red Line Statement:** Jesus was falsely accused and sentenced to death on a cross, yet He continued to bear witness to the truth.

- **Red Line Connection:** Jesus came to bear witness to the truth so that all might know that He is the fulfillment of God's promise of a Messiah.

- **Focal Passage:** John 18:28–40

 Listen Attentively to the Lesson

1. Tell the story of John 18:28–40 in your own words.

   Context: On the night of Jesus' arrest, Judas came to the garden of Gethsemane to betray Jesus, accompanied by an armed detachment of troops and officers from the chief priests and Pharisees (18:3). The troops led Jesus first to Annas, the father-in-law of the high priest Caiaphas (18:13). When Caiaphas questioned Jesus, the scribes and elders were assembled. The Jewish leaders had prepared people to give false testimony against Jesus. The high priest brought the proceedings to a head when he demanded that Jesus tell them if He was the Son of God, the Christ. When Jesus affirmed that He was the Christ, the chief priest flew into a rage for what he called blasphemy, and the assembly said that Jesus was deserving of death. They spat in Jesus' face, beat Him, and mocked Him (Matthew 26:57–68). They were ready for Jesus to die, but they would have to wait until morning to proceed with their plan. The Jews had considered Jesus and rejected Him as the Messiah, but the Roman government would also have to grapple with the identity of Jesus.

2. Reconstruct John 18:28–40 together, including as many details as your small group remembers.

3. Read the passage aloud together from Scripture, confirming the facts of the story. Amend any details suggested by small-group members that did not accurately represent the Scripture.

Investigate the Facts of the Lesson

Use these questions to guide small-group members to investigate the facts of this passage.

1. The Jews wouldn't enter the Praetorium where Pilate lived; they wanted to stay undefiled so they could partake of the Passover meal (v. 28). What is the irony of their false thinking about staying "clean"? How were the Jewish leaders fooling themselves about defilement?

   They were already defiled because of the wretched sin in their hearts. The night before, they had beaten and mocked the true Passover Lamb; now they were trying to stay ceremonially clean in order to eat the Passover, a worshipful celebration that pointed to Jesus, the Lamb who would be slain to save everyone who would believe in Him from eternal death.

2. Pilate played a major role in God's fulfillment of His plan for Jesus to be crucified.

a. Was Pilate eager to put Jesus on trial (vv. 31, 38)? Read Luke 23:2, which records the three accusations the Jews made against Jesus in order to peak Pilate's interest. Which accusation seemed to matter to Pilate?

Pilate preferred that the Jews handle their dispute with Jesus according to Jewish law, leaving the Roman government out of the situation. Luke 23:2 records that the Jews accused Jesus of perverting the nation, forbidding payment of taxes to Caesar, and claiming to be a king. It is the last accusation that seemed to be of most interest to Pilate.

b. What kind of man was Pilate? How did he respond to the pressure of this situation?

History records that the time of Passover was usually a tense time in Jerusalem during the days of Roman rule, and the Roman government kept a close watch for Jewish uprisings as masses of Jews swelled the city. Allow your small group to share their thoughts on Pilate. He appeared to be uncomfortable with condemning Jesus because he thought Jesus was innocent, but Pilate was also unwilling to make the Jewish mob angry. Because Jesus was a Galilean, Pilate even attempted at one point to pass off the situation to Herod, who had jurisdiction in Galilee, but Herod sent Jesus back to Pilate (Luke 23:6–12).

3. What other details do you see in this passage?

Allow your small group to share other details that stand out to them and discuss the significance of each point.

Find the purpose of the lesson

Use these questions to guide small-group members to discover God's purpose for the passage.

1. Jesus did not allow this time of questioning from Pilate to be a formality. How did Jesus draw Pilate personally into the debate in verse 34? Why would Jesus want to cause Pilate to grapple personally with whether or not He was King of the Jews?

    Jesus took what could have been a formality, a stepping stone to the Cross, and turned it into an opportunity to proclaim the truth to Pilate, a man who needed a personal Savior. To the very end, Jesus was pointing people to the truth.

2. What did Jesus mean when He explained to Pilate that He was indeed a King, but clarified that His kingdom is not of this world (v. 36)?

    Possible answer: Jesus' authority to reign doesn't come from powerful men or the will of the majority on earth. Jesus' authority to reign wasn't initiated by brute force through manmade weaponry. Jesus' kingdom is established through the authority of God. His kingdom is spiritual and far superior to the kingdoms of this world. Point out to your small group that while His kingdom is not of this world, Jesus reigns in this world in the hearts of all who have surrendered their lives to Him. Our citizenship is not of this world (Philippians 3:20).

3. Truth is an important theme of Jesus' conversation with Pilate.

    a. What specific reason did Jesus give for why He was born and why He had come into this world (v. 37)?

    Jesus said the reason was for Him to bear witness to the truth. In other passages, Jesus spoke of other reasons for His coming (for instance,

John 3:16–17), but Jesus was very clear with Pilate that He had come to declare to mankind what is true.

b. What did Jesus say about people who hear His voice (v. 37)? Why do people have such a difficult time recognizing the truth?

People of the truth hear His voice. People of the truth can recognize truth when it is spoken, and they know the voice of Jesus like a sheep recognizes the voice of its shepherd. People who don't walk with Christ have no foundation, no basis for truth. Ask your small group why Christians also struggle at times with discerning what is true.

c. In a world where a war is raging over what is the truth, what does it mean to you that you can depend on hearing the voice of Jesus, reaffirming the truth to you?

Allow everyone to respond.

4. Jesus has said, "I am the way, and the truth, and the life" (John 14:6). Pilate was looking into the eyes of the Son of God, the Christ, the Messiah, the One who is truth. Pilate asked Jesus, "What is truth?", but he didn't wait long enough for Jesus to answer.

a. What is your source of truth, both in what you believe is true and also where you look for answers when you're seeking the truth?

Allow your small group to respond.

b. Have you learned to have the patience needed to wait upon the Lord when you ask Him to reveal truth in your life?

Be prepared to share an answer from your own experience. Remind everyone that Jesus said that we who are of the truth hear His voice.

c. Many people in the world are searching for answers. They want to know the truth. How would you describe to someone that Jesus is the truth?

Allow everyone to express how God has revealed the truth to them. Encourage each person to be ready to share with others about Jesus as the way, the truth, and the life.

5. What other truths from this passage stand out to you? What else can we learn about God or learn about being a follower of Christ?

Allow everyone to respond. Share any other points of spiritual growth that the Holy Spirit brings to your attention.

Experience the Truth of the Lesson

Use these questions to guide small-group members to allow God's transformational truths to reshape their hearts and minds.

1. The Jews rejected Jesus as their Messiah and delivered Him over to Pilate, but it was the Roman government that agreed to crucify Jesus. The Jews beat Jesus and mocked and spit upon Him, and the Romans severely abused Him with scourging, mocking, spitting, and beating (Matthew 27:26–31). Who takes the blame for the crucifixion of Jesus Christ?

Allow your small group to discuss the role of both the corrupt Jewish leaders and cruel Romans (representatives of the Gentile world) in Jesus' crucifixion. (You may want to refer to Acts 2:23.) Then ask your small group to consider their own culpability in Jesus' crucifixion. How are we also to blame for the crucifixion?

2. Pilate put a choice before the Jews: Barabbas or Jesus? Barabbas was a robber (John 18:40), a notorious prisoner (Matthew 27:16), and a murdering insurrectionist (Luke 23:19). The people who were calling for Jesus' crucifixion were saying that they would rather put up with Barabbas on the streets than have Jesus in their lives. God always calls us to choose between Him and the world. Think about a situation you're currently facing and try to find a fresh perspective—how can you boil that situation down to a choice you'll have to make between Jesus and the world?

It seems unthinkable to us that anyone would choose Barabbas over Jesus, but we face these same kinds of choices every day: pornography or Jesus? Lying or Jesus? Gossip or Jesus? Adultery or Jesus? Selfishness or Jesus? Challenge your small group to put themselves in the crowd that day, and put their temptation to sin in the place of Barabbas. Will they choose Jesus or that sin? Mankind often chooses sin, yet Jesus gave His life for us, the ones who so often reject Him. You may choose to end your lesson by reading Matthew 27:22–25, a powerful passage with another great reminder that Jesus' crucifixion traces back on the thin red line of redemption for the Jews and for the world.

101

Between the Lines: Truth Points

Praetorium (v. 28)—from the Greek military word *praitorion*, denoting a governor's residence or a general's tent or headquarters. In this passage, "Praetorium" denotes Pilate's residence. In ancient Rome, the praetor was a senior magistrate responsible for administrating civil justice.

Defiled (v. 28)—ceremonially unclean.

Pilate (v. 29)—Pontius Pilate was the Roman governor in Judea from AD 26–36. He served directly under Caesar. His position gave him the authority from Rome to grant life or death to the population in his jurisdiction.

"Judge Him according to your law" (v. 31)—Scripture indicates that the Jewish method of capital punishment was by stoning. However, God had ordained that Jesus would die, not by stoning, but by crucifixion (Deuteronomy 21:22–23; John 3:14, 8:28, 12:32–33; Galatians 3:13).

> *A man who can read the New Testament and not see that Christ claims to be more than a man, can look all over the sky at high noon on a cloudless day and not see the sun.*
>
> WILLIAM E. BIEDERWOLF

FULFILLMENT OF GOD'S PROMISE

- **Red Line Verse:** *"He is not here, for He has risen, just as He said."* (Matthew 28:6)

- **Red Line Statement:** Jesus suffered and died on the Cross, and then three days later, rose in victory from the dead. Jesus conquered death and paid mankind's sin debt.

- **Red Line Connection:** Jesus Christ is the fulfillment of God's promised Savior of the world.

- **Background Passage:** Matthew 27:27–28:8

- **Focal Passages:** Matthew 27:35–46; 28:1–8

 Listen Attentively to the Lesson

1. Tell the story of Matthew 27:35–46 in your own words.

    Context: Jesus had already suffered an unfair trial and the brutality of the Jewish leaders on Thursday night, followed by questioning by Pilate, rejection by the people, and scourging by the Romans on Friday morning. Jesus' body was already mangled from the beatings and the crown of thorns, but the time had come for Jesus to suffer and die on the Cross at Calvary.

2. Reconstruct Matthew 27:35–46 together, including as many details as your small group remembers.

3. Read the passage aloud together from Scripture, confirming the facts of the story. Amend any details suggested by small-group members that did not accurately represent the Scripture.

Investigate the Facts of the Lesson

Use these questions to guide small-group members to investigate the facts of this passage.

1. Many people, both Romans and Jews, were eyewitnesses to Jesus' crucifixion.

   a. Were the people able to comprehend the Son of God hanging from a cross?

   To the passersby, Jesus appeared to be weak and defeated, not the Son of God. The Cross seemed to prove to them that Jesus was not who He claimed to be.

   b. The people mocked Jesus for His comments about the Temple being destroyed and rebuilt in three days (27:40). How was Jesus actually fulfilling what He had said (John 2:19–22)?

   Jesus was speaking figuratively about Himself, not the Temple building. Jesus' body was being destroyed through the beatings and crucifixion. Three days later He would rise from the dead.

   c. The chief priests, scribes, and elders mocked Jesus, speaking of how Jesus could save others but not save Himself, as if the trial, beatings, and crucifixion overwhelmed Jesus (27:42). What had these men failed to understand about how Jesus saves people?

   Jesus was laying down His life in order to save mankind for all of eternity. Jesus wasn't overcome by the crucifixion; it simply was not His purpose to save Himself.

2. The crowds made taunting statements to Jesus such as, "If you are the Son of God..." (27:40), and "If He is the King of Israel..." (27:42 NKJV).

   a. How do these statements from the crowd relate to the types of statements the devil made when he tempted Jesus in the wilderness (Matthew 4:3–6)?

   The devil also tried to manipulate Jesus by daring Him to prove His deity by doing things that were contrary to the will of the Father.

   b. Did the crowds need more proof from Jesus that He was the Messiah?

   Allow everyone to respond. Certainly Jesus had performed many miracles and taught with authority among them. His love and truth were amazing, and many had already placed their faith in Jesus. He had given much proof that He was the Christ and His life fulfilled every prophecy, but God also requires that we come to Him by faith, not by proof.

   c. How do the actions, words, and attitudes of the Jews as they watched Jesus dying on the Cross compare to the actions, words, and attitudes that the children of Israel had displayed throughout history as God reached out to His people?

   Allow your small group to draw the similarities they notice. Just as in times past in the history of the Jews, a small remnant of Jews were faithful to God even on the day of the crucifixion, watching their Lord suffer and die.

3. The two thieves being crucified with Jesus were so filled with hate that they were even willing to use up some of their waning energy to hurl insults at Jesus (vv. 38, 44). However, one of those thieves changed his mind about Jesus and was offered salvation by Christ from the Cross (Luke 23:39–43). How does the story of

the thieves show how depraved mankind can be and how merciful and loving God is?

The thieves on the Cross, convicted and suffering the penalty of a cruel death, were still so deceived and filled with hate that they spent their final moments not reflecting on their own sin but instead trying to inflict more pain on someone else. What a horrible picture of how evil mankind can be! But one thief was converted by seeing the way Jesus conducted Himself during the crucifixion. Amazingly he was changed, and Jesus loved him enough to offer him forgiveness in his final moments before death. What a beautiful picture of God's mercy!

4. What other details do you see in this passage?

    Allow your small group to share other details that stand out to them and discuss the significance of each point.

Find the purpose of the lesson

Use these questions to guide small-group members to discover God's purpose for the passage.

1. Many people were there at the Cross to observe Jesus' death. In arrogance, they discussed His claims and questioned His authority. Even today, people continue to evaluate Jesus and inspect His death and resurrection story. What does the world demand from Jesus if they are to believe in Him? Why do people reject the notion of a Savior dying on a cross?

    Possible answer: The world cries out for absolute proof, and it wants God to produce proof or "signs" on demand. People often struggle with the concept of Jesus on the Cross because they think of Jesus as weak and defeated. They don't understand the power, will, and strength that Jesus displayed by choosing to submit Himself to such agony and humiliation at the hands of His creation.

2. When Jesus cried out in verse 46 (quoting Psalm 22:1), He was expressing the horrible experience of feeling separated from the Father because He was carrying the sins of all mankind. Do you remember a time in your life when you realized that your sin had created a barrier between you and God?

Be prepared to share from your own life experience. Nothing can separate us from the love of God (Romans 8:39), but sin separates us from fellowship with Him (Isaiah 59:2).

3. When Jesus died, the veil of the Temple miraculously was torn in two from the top to the bottom (vv. 50–51). This veil separated mankind from the holiest of holy places in the Temple, symbolically separating mankind from God. How does this removal of the veil symbolize what Jesus did on the Cross?

We now have access to God through Jesus Christ! We may enter boldly into His throne room because we have a relationship with Jesus (Hebrews 10:19–20). He conquered sin, and we have no need for the Temple or the altar of sacrifice; we are the Temple of God (1 Corinthians 6:19). Jesus was the perfect sacrifice, and we're called to be living sacrifices (Romans 12:1).

4. What other truths from this passage stand out to you? What else can we learn about God or learn about being a follower of Christ?

Allow everyone to respond. Share any other points of spiritual growth that the Holy Spirit brings to your attention.

Experience the Truth of the Lesson

Use these questions to guide small-group members to allow God's transformational truths to reshape their hearts and minds.

1. We can't experience the truth of the Crucifixion without celebrating the reality of the Resurrection. Read Matthew 28:1–8.

a. Who was first to hear the news of Jesus' Resurrection? Why not someone "more important"?

Mary ("the other Mary," not the mother of Jesus) and Mary Magdalene were first to hear. Jesus could have appeared to the eleven disciples first, but the honor went to women who were being faithful to honor the Lord by going to anoint His body with spices (Mark 16:1). It is also another proof of the reliability of Scripture. If someone had invented the Resurrection accounts, the writer would not have had women, whose testimony was considered untrustworthy and was inadmissible in first century courts, as the first witnesses. By choosing these women instead of men of influence, God showed how much He values every person, regardless of gender or position in this world or in ministry. God is no respecter of persons; we are all important to God, and we all have a voice to share the good news—Jesus is risen!

b. The women were expecting to find the dead body of Jesus; they even wondered how they would roll the stone away (Mark 16:3). They didn't remember that Jesus had promised to rise again after three days. However, the chief priests and Pharisees remembered, and they convinced Pilate to allow them to set a guard at the tomb because they feared what might happen (Matthew 27:62–66). Why would Christ's enemies remember this detail but not Christ's followers? What are the instances in your life when you sometimes forget Christ's promises?

Allow your small group to respond.

c. Jesus didn't need an angel to roll the stone away for Him; He had already been resurrected. Why did God send an angel to remove the stone? How was this an act of compassion toward us?

The stone was rolled away so that Jesus' followers could see the grave-clothes and the empty tomb. This proof of Jesus' resurrection was another act of compassion toward us. God didn't have to offer us proof of the Resurrection, but He chose to let us peek inside the tomb to strengthen our faith.

2. When you think about Christ's death and resurrection, what is the word that you would use to describe what God has done for you?

    Allow your small group to share what the death and resurrection of Jesus means to them.

3. Why must the stories of the Crucifixion and the Resurrection be told together?

    The two acts together are the completion of God's gift to mankind. Encourage everyone to understand and embrace both the Crucifixion and the Resurrection stories.

4. Examine Philippians 3:10. What would you ask of God this week so that you may better know Christ and the power of His resurrection? If it requires conforming to His death and partaking of His sufferings, are you willing to surrender all to gain a deeper walk with Jesus Christ?

    Ask your small group to encourage one another this week to experience Christ's death and resurrection in a new and living way.

Between the Lines: Truth Points

Casting lots (27:35)—Lots were objects used much like our dice of today. Casting lots was often done as a fair means to determine the will of God (or in the case of the pagan world, the will of "the gods," see Proverbs 16:33). A New Testament example of casting lots is the disciples' selection process to replace Judas Iscariot as the twelfth disciple (Acts 1:26).

Sixth hour until the ninth hour (27:45)—about noon until 3 p.m.

Sabbath (28:1)—The Jewish day began at sundown on the previous day; thus the Sabbath officially began on Friday evening at sundown.

Mary Magdalene and the other Mary (28:1)—According to Mark's account, the other Mary was the mother of James (Mark 16:1). Both women were followers of Jesus and witnessed the Crucifixion (Matthew 27:56).

Guards (28:4)—With Pilate's permission, the Pharisees and chief priests placed a guard at Jesus' tomb and sealed the stone at the entrance (27:62–66). The Jewish leaders bribed the guards to lie about what happened at the tomb (28:11–15).

> *The devil has convinced so many people that they are worthless.*
> *Each of us needs to stop and remember the cross—at the cross we*
> *will discover our true value— for it is here that we discover the*
> *price God was willing to pay for us, the depth of His love, and*
> *how much we are worth to Him.* ROY LESSIN

LIFE LESSON 39

Jesus' Last Days on Earth

Red Line Verse: *"Were not our hearts burning within us while He was speaking to us on the road, while He was explaining the Scriptures to us?"* (Luke 24:32)

Red Line Statement: After His resurrection, Jesus appeared to many people and helped them understand why He had suffered and died for their sins.

Red Line Connection: Many eyewitnesses testified of the risen Jesus.

Focal Passage: Luke 24:13–35

Listen Attentively to the Lesson

1. Tell the story of Luke 24:13–35 in your own words.

   Context: Following the Resurrection, Jesus "presented Himself alive after His suffering, by many convincing proofs, appearing to (the apostles) over a period of forty days and speaking of the things concerning the kingdom of God" (Acts 1:3). All four gospels contain accounts of these appearances and also the struggles of disbelief the disciples experienced. Mark recorded that Jesus "appeared to the eleven themselves as they were reclining at the table; and He reproached them for their unbelief and hardness of heart, because they had not believed those who had seen Him after He had risen" (Mark 16:14). Two such men who met the risen Savior had the blessing of walking with Him on the Emmaus Road.

2. Reconstruct Luke 24:13–35 together, including as many details as your small group remembers.

3. Read the passage aloud together from Scripture, confirming the facts of the story. Amend any details suggested by small-group members that did not accurately represent the Scripture.

 Investigate the Facts of the Lesson
Use these questions to guide small-group members to investigate the facts of this passage.

1. What were the two disciples discussing on the road, and how were they feeling (vv. 17–18)?

    The Greek words used in this verse mean they were examining and seeking. As they discussed Jesus and the events that had occurred over the past three days, they were filled with sadness.

2. When they told Jesus what had happened, what facts did they seem sure about? What details or events were they unsure about (vv. 19–24)?

    They were confident about Jesus' ministry and His crucifixion, but they expressed no confidence in the resurrection. Ask your small group why the two disciples were so resistant to believe in the testimony from the other Christ followers; was it because they hadn't seen the risen Savior with their own eyes? Why didn't they believe the testimony of others?

3. What did Cleopas admit that they had hoped Jesus was going to do (v. 21)?

They hoped He would redeem Israel. Indeed Jesus did redeem Israel, but not in a political sense as some of the Jews had expected. The price of redemption was paid through Jesus' shed blood on the Cross and had nothing to do with overthrowing the Roman government. Jesus came to redeem man's soul.

4. After Jesus had gone home with them and had broken the bread and then disappeared from their sight, what did the two men do (v. 33)? How important was this event in the life of these two men?

They backtracked several miles to Jerusalem to tell the other disciples that "the Lord has really risen" (v. 34)!

113

5. What other details do you see in this passage?

Allow your small group to share other details that stand out to them and discuss the significance of each point.

Find the purpose of the lesson

Use these questions to guide small-group members to discover God's purpose for the passage.

1. These two disciples were talking over every detail, trying to settle in their minds just what had taken place with Jesus. How had Jesus' crucifixion personally affected all of His disciples? What kinds of questions might the disciples have been dealing with between the time of Jesus' crucifixion and when they knew that Jesus had risen from the dead?

The disciples had placed their hope in Jesus as Messiah and, upon His death, they may have been asking themselves, "What next?" Their life direction

*had been set toward following Jesus, so they probably were feeling shock,
confusion, and deep pain. Ask your small group, "Have you ever had an
event happen in your life unexpectedly that really shook your foundation and
caused you to lose your direction?"*

2. After Cleopas explained what had happened, it was Jesus' turn to
speak.

   a. According to verse 25, what was the blind spot of the disciples?
   As you think about what these disciples had expected the
   Messiah to do, what is the significance of the word "all"?

      *Jesus said they had failed to believe in all that the prophets had spoken
      about the coming Messiah. They had embraced the prophecies about a
      coming King who would redeem Israel, but they failed to understand the
      many prophecies about Jesus' suffering and death, that He would be as a
      lamb led to slaughter. Jesus had prophesied about His suffering and death,
      but the disciples hadn't absorbed His words.*

   b. As we grow as Christians, why is it important that we accept *all*
   that the Bible teaches us about who Jesus is and what it means
   to be a Christian? Why can't we focus just on the blessings of
   being a Christian and ignore the challenging aspects of being
   a follower of Christ? What is the danger in reading only those
   passages of Scripture that make us feel comfortable or that we
   can easily understand?

      *When we pick and choose what we want to embrace of Christianity,
      we will be disillusioned and ill-equipped when the reality of suffering and
      sacrifice for Christ comes. All of God's Word is significant, and every
      teaching is important. When we avoid portions of Scripture for our personal
      study, we will having gaping holes in our understanding of who God is and
      what it means to follow Christ.*

c. Jesus began at Moses and taught the men how the Scriptures related to Him (v. 27). Jesus pointed them to the *thin red line!* From your "Thin Red Line" studies in the Old Testament (if your small group has completed volumes 1 and 2), what are some of the stories Jesus may have told the two men that pointed to the coming Messiah?

Be prepared to share your own ideas as your small group shares. If your small group has completed volumes 1 and 2, ask what their "Emmaus Road" experience was like as they studied through the Old Testament in those 26 lessons. What did Jesus teach them about Himself?

3. If Jesus had revealed Himself to the two men when He first met them on the road, perhaps they would have been so shocked that they wouldn't have listened as carefully to Him explaining from Scripture what had been prophesied about the Messiah. Jesus gave them a working knowledge of Scripture to help them better understand God's plan from the beginning.

a. We often emphasize faith in Christ, and faith is essential to being a Christian. But on the Emmaus Road, Jesus gave value to knowing the evidence in Scripture that points to Jesus as Messiah. How do we as Christians balance faith in Jesus Christ and proof of Jesus as the Christ? Are you comfortable with pointing people to the evidence that Jesus is the Christ?

Because God's Word teaches us that we are saved by grace through faith (Ephesians 2:8), you may have small-group members who have never had interest in the scriptural evidence that points to Jesus as the Christ. Share Romans 10:17 which gives a great description of the connection between faith and God's Word. Encourage your small group to think about what evidence they already know and to feel comfortable sharing it with others. We come to Christ through faith, but God has given us evidence that strengthens our faith and helps us share the truth with others.

b. How did the two disciples describe their experience with Jesus in verse 32? Is it possible to have that same experience when you open God's Word? Does God still offer to be the One to explain Scripture to us?

Their hearts burned within them as Jesus taught them. We can have that same experience today of being taught by God, and in fact, the Holy Spirit is our Teacher (John 14:26). Ask your small group to share openly about their times of Scripture study—do they sense God's presence? Are they excited about God's Word? Do their hearts "burn" like the two disciples? Encourage your small group to read God's Word daily, and to ask the Holy Spirit to be their Teacher.

4. What other truths from this passage stand out to you? What else can we learn about God or learn about being a follower of Christ?

Allow everyone to respond. Share any other points of spiritual growth that the Holy Spirit brings to your attention.

Experience the Truth of the Lesson

Use these questions to guide small-group members to allow God's transformational truths to reshape their hearts and minds.

1. It wasn't until He broke the bread that the two men were able to recognize Jesus (vv. 30–31).

a. How would you describe the love Jesus had for these two men? How did Jesus express His love for them through this experience?

Jesus loved them enough to walk this road with them and thoroughly explain Scripture to them. He gave them a life-changing gift.

b. Has God ever allowed you to journey a difficult road in order to teach you valuable lessons along the way? How did you know that Jesus was with you? What happened when you got to the end of that life experience and God let you know that He was there all the time?

   As your small group shares, rejoice with each person that God teaches us lessons in our life journeys, God is faithful to be with us, and He strengthens our faith.

2. We don't know exactly how long the two men traveled with Jesus, but the journey was long enough for the Lord to teach them profound truths from Scripture. Do you long for an Emmaus Road experience with God? Would you be willing to set aside one full hour this week to sit quietly with your Bible and allow God to be your teacher?

   Encourage your small-group members to make this commitment to each other.

Betweent the Lines: Truth Points

Emmaus (v. 13)—a small village eight miles northwest of Jerusalem.

Cleopas (v. 18)—one of the followers of Jesus who associated with Jesus' disciples. Cleopas is only mentioned in this passage of Scripture.

Some women (v. 22)—Mary Magdalene and Mary spoke with the angel at the empty tomb and also met Jesus (Matthew 28:1–10).

Mark's account records that Salome was also present (Mark 16:1) and that Mary Magdalene was the first to see the risen Savior (16:9). Luke 24:10 names Joanna and also notes that "other women" gave testimony to the disciples about what happened at the tomb.

Breaking of bread (v. 30)—The breaking of bread was a common meal activity for the Jews.

> *The entire plan for the future has its key in the resurrection.*
>
> BILLY GRAHAM

WEEKLY PREPARATION FOR SMALL-GROUP MEMBERS

Would your small-group members like to prepare for each week's lesson? Consider these two options.

OPTION 1: A Private Walk with God

When we learn to open God's Word and let the Holy Spirit be our Teacher, God can pierce our hearts with the specific truths that are relevant to our daily needs. With the "A Private Walk with God" option, each small-group member is invited to take a private walk with God through the Scripture, friend to friend, for one-on-one time alone with God. Imagine how each person will grow, draw near to God, and deepen their love for the Word when they hear the words of God falling personally upon their own ear. One Teacher, one student.

Provide the "A Private Walk with God" tool for each small-group member, encouraging them to keep the tool tucked in their Bible for easy reference. Each week, provide the focal passage for the upcoming lesson to your small group, and ask small-group members to read through the passage using these questions, recording their reflections in a notebook or journal. In your weekly small-group discussions, commend the efforts of those who are contributing to the discussion based on how God has spoken to them through their "A Private Walk with God" weekly preparation.

THIN RED LINE

Find a quiet place to sit alone with your Bible, a notebook or journal, and the following set of questions. Each week, read through the focal passage several times, and ask God to be your personal Teacher, and you His student. Pray for personal insights and life application as well as biblical knowledge. Enjoy this time alone with God! Every child of God can hear His voice speaking to us directly from the Scriptures; we need only to listen. Whether in a thundering voice or a gentle whisper, He will speak to you.

As for you, the anointing which you received from Him abides in you, and you have no need for anyone to teach you; but as His anointing teaches you about all things, and is true and is not a lie, and just as it has taught you, you abide in Him. (1 John 2:27)

1. What are the key words that stand out to you in this passage?

2. What is the main idea of this passage? Is there more than one theme?

3. What does this passage reveal about who God is?

4. What does this passage reveal about what it means to be a disciple of Christ?

5. Is there a truth or a phrase from this passage that is particularly meaningful to you in your current life circumstances? How can this truth or phrase strengthen your walk with Christ?

6. Is there a word, phrase, or verse that you have questions about? If so, write down your questions. Pray and ask the Holy Spirit to increase your understanding. Read the passage again.

7. Ask God to help you apply the truths of this passage today. If this time of study has brought to mind any prayer requests you can bring to God about your friends, family, church, nation, or world, talk with God about these prayer concerns.

OPTION 2: Awaken Your Mind

Provide a copy of the printable "Awaken Your Mind" small-group member preparation guide. You may choose to incorporate these additional questions into your weekly small-group time, or another option is to encourage your small group to engage in online discussions of these questions in preparation for your small-group gathering.

THE BIRTH OF OUR LORD

Red Line Verse: *"She will bear a Son; and you shall call His name Jesus, for He will save His people from their sins."* (Matthew 1:21)

Red Line Statement: God's promises are fulfilled in Jesus Christ, the Messiah, who came to save us from our sins.

Red Line Connection: In times past, God sent human deliverers and leaders to rescue His people from their enemies; when God sent His Son, He sent the ultimate Deliverer. Jesus sets us free from the power of sin.

Background Passage: Matthew 1–2

Focal Passage: Matthew 1:18–2:12

Questions to Consider:

1. What are the names ascribed to Mary's Son in this passage (1:18, 21, 23; 2:2, 4, 6)?

2. Compare Joseph's experience with Mary's encounter with Gabriel in Luke 1:26–38.

3. Why did the wise men want to find the King of the Jews (2:2)? Why did Herod want to find Him?

4. How did the wise men respond when they finally met Jesus (2:10–11)?

FOLLOWING THE EXAMPLE OF JESUS

- **Red Line Verse:** *"Why is it that you were looking for Me? Did you not know that I had to be in My Father's house?"* (Luke 2:49)

- **Red Line Statement:** Jesus came to fulfill the will of His Father and, even as a youth, He remained focused on His calling.

- **Red Line Connection:** Jesus Christ willingly came to the earth to give His entire life in sacrifice for us according to God's perfect plan.

- **Focal Passage:** Luke 2:40–52

123

Questions to Consider:

1. How do Jesus' actions, focus, and words reflect His awareness of who He was?

2. How would you tell this story from the perspective of the teachers in the Temple?

3. How would you tell this story from the perspective of Mary and Joseph?

4. How does Luke 2:52 compare to the growth you're currently experiencing in your life?

TEMPTED YET VICTORIOUS

Red Line Verse: *For we do not have a high priest who cannot sympathize with our weaknesses, but One who has been tempted in all things as we are, yet without sin.* (Hebrews 4:15)

Red Line Statement: Jesus took on flesh and faced temptation, but He was victorious over temptation and remained without sin.

Red Line Connection: Jesus can sympathize with our struggles with temptation because He, too, was tempted. His victory gives us hope that we can also be victorious over sin.

Focal Passage: Luke 4:1–13

Questions to Consider:

1. What were the circumstances in this story that put Jesus in a weakened state as One who was not only fully God but also fully man (vv. 1–2)?

2. How did Jesus respond to each temptation (vv. 4, 8, 12)?

3. How do the devil's tactics against Jesus compare to the ways he tries to tempt you?

4. By successfully undergoing this temptation, what has Jesus taught us about how to defeat the enemy?

Jesus Calls Us to Serve Him

Red Line Verse: *Philip found Nathanael and said to him, "We have found Him of whom Moses in the Law and also the Prophets wrote—Jesus of Nazareth, the son of Joseph."* (John 1:45)

Red Line Statement: Jesus invested particularly in the lives of 12 men, training them to be disciples of Christ and to make disciples of others.

Red Line Connection: Each of us who follow Christ have a role to play on God's thin red line of redemption as we serve as disciples and we make disciples for Christ.

Focal Passage: John 1:35–51

Questions to Consider:

1. What did John the Baptist do that caused his disciples to follow Jesus (vv. 35–37)?

2. What did Andrew do to help his brother find Jesus the Messiah (vv. 40–42)?

3. Why was Nathanael skeptical about Jesus (v. 46)?

4. What convinced Nathanael that Jesus was the Son of God (vv. 47–49)? Why are you convinced that Jesus is God's Son?

Preaching God's Message

- **Red Line Verse:** *"Blessed are the pure in heart, for they shall see God."* (Matthew 5:8)

- **Red Line Statement:** Jesus taught us how to experience God's blessings by exercising the godly character God instills in followers of Christ.

- **Red Line Connection:** Only through Christ are we able to fulfill His great teachings.

- **Focal Passage:** Matthew 5:1–12

Questions to Consider:

1. Which of these teachings of Christ do you find most challenging to fulfill? Why?

2. What is the good news to those who are persecuted for the sake of Christ (vv. 10–12)?

3. How does the fruit of the Spirit (Galatians 5:22–23) relate to Jesus' teachings in the Beatitudes?

4. Which of these promised blessings of Christ means the most to you? Why?

DISPLAYING GOD'S POWER

- **Red Line Verse:** *Those who were in the boat worshipped Him, saying, "You are certainly God's Son!"* (Matthew 14:33)

- **Red Line Statement:** Jesus performed many miracles that displayed His power and authority as the Son of God.

- **Red Line Connection:** Jesus revealed Himself as the Messiah and Son of God so that mankind might follow Him and be saved.

- **Focal Passage:** Matthew 14:22–33

127

Questions to Consider:

1. Look back to Matthew 14:13–21. What had the disciples just experienced with Jesus before they got into the boat?

2. How would you describe the life lesson Jesus wanted to teach the disciples on the water that night?

3. What was Peter's triumph in this story? What was his failure?

4. Consider what Jesus said the three times He spoke in this passage. Read His words in verses 27, 29, and 31 as if Jesus is saying these words directly to you. What is your response?

JESUS SHOWS CARE AND CONCERN

Red Line Verse: *And He said to her, "Daughter, your faith has made you well; go in peace."* (Luke 8:48)

Red Line Statement: Jesus showed compassion for the suffering by healing the sick and raising the dead. He displayed His authority over death and His life-giving power.

Red Line Connection: The Son of God has power to give us hope, healing, and life.

Focal Passage: Luke 8:40–56

Questions to Consider:

1. Instead of addressing Jesus face to face to ask for healing, how did the woman with the hemorrhage approach Jesus for healing (v. 44)?

2. What did Peter say to Jesus to indicate that he didn't realize what was happening on the road to Jairus's house (v. 45)?

3. What effect might the woman's testimony of healing have had on the crowds?

4. How have you experienced the power of Jesus Christ to bring you from death unto life?

Jesus Is Messiah

- **Red Line Verse:** *"You are the Christ, the Son of the Living God."* (Matthew 16:16)

- **Red Line Statement:** Knowing the time was approaching for Him to suffer and die on the Cross, Jesus prepared His disciples to stand firmly on the truth that He was the Christ.

- **Red Line Connection:** Jesus knew He was the Christ and wanted others to know.

- **Focal Passage:** Matthew 16:13–20

129

Questions to Consider:

1. Since Jesus knew all things, why do you think Jesus asked the disciples what people were saying about His identity (v. 13)?

2. What insight did Jesus give us about how a person comes to faith in Jesus as Christ, the Son of the living God (v. 17)?

3. What are the promises Jesus spoke to Peter (vv. 18–19), and what do these promises mean to us as Christians today?

4. Read Matthew 16:21–17:13. How was Jesus preparing His disciples for His death and resurrection?

The King Has Come

Red Line Verse: *The crowds going ahead of Him, and those who followed, were shouting, "Hosanna to the Son of David; Blessed is He who comes in the name of the LORD; Hosanna in the highest!"* (Matthew 21:9)

Red Line Statement: Jesus made His identity as King of kings and Messiah known when He entered into Jerusalem mounted on a colt, receiving the praise of the Jews.

Red Line Connection: Jesus is the One and only rightful heir to the throne of David. He is the fulfillment of God's promises to the Jews as King of kings.

130

Focal Passage: Matthew 21:1–11

Questions to Consider:

1. What details of this event point to Jesus as the King of kings and the promised Messiah of Israel?

2. Because of Jesus' entry on the colt, what were people talking about in Jerusalem (v. 10)?

3. What further details of this event do you find in the other Gospel accounts (Mark 11:1–10; Luke 19:28–40; John 12:12–19)?

4. Based on John 12:16, how would you describe the events of the triumphal entry from the disciples' perspective?

FINAL MOMENTS BEFORE THE ARREST

Red Line Verse: *"For this is My blood of the covenant, which is poured out for many for forgiveness of sins."* (Matthew 26:28)

Red Line Statement: Jesus ate the Passover with His disciples and instituted communion as a remembrance of Christ's life given as a new covenant between God and mankind.

Red Line Connection: Jesus was the sacrificial Lamb of God whose body was broken and blood shed to give us a new covenant with God.

Focal Passages: Matthew 26:20–30, 36–42

Questions to Consider:

1. When Jesus told the disciples that one of them would betray Him, how was that a display of Jesus' authority over His impending arrest and crucifixion?

2. How do Jesus' words in verse 24 show us the amazing way God's sovereignty connects with mankind's free will to make choices?

3. From the scene in the garden, do you relate more to Jesus or to Peter, James, and John in the way you approach prayer?

4. God chose to allow us to know how Jesus prayed in the garden. What does Jesus' prayer to the Father teach you about prayer (v. 39, 42)?

ACCEPTING OR REJECTING JESUS

Red Line Verse: *Jesus answered, "You say correctly that I am a king. For this I have been born, and for this I have come into the world, to testify to the truth. Everyone who is of the truth hears My voice."* (John 18:37)

Red Line Statement: Jesus was falsely accused and sentenced to death on a cross, yet He continued to bear witness to the truth.

Red Line Connection: Jesus came to bear witness to the truth so that all might know that He is the fulfillment of God's promise of a Messiah.

Focal Passage: John 18:28–40

Questions to Consider:

1. Why did the Jewish leaders want Jesus to be prosecuted by Pilate instead of handling the situation on their own (v. 31)?

2. What did Pilate ask Jesus (vv. 33, 35, 37, 38)? If Pilate's heart had been open, how could the answer to any of these questions have been enough to point Pilate to salvation?

3. What reason did Jesus give for why He came to the earth (v. 37)?

4. Who is responsible for Jesus' crucifixion?

FULFILLMENT OF GOD'S PROMISE

- **Red Line Verse:** *"He is not here, for He has risen, just as He said."* (Matthew 28:6)

- **Red Line Statement:** Jesus suffered and died on the Cross, and then three days later, rose in victory from the dead. Jesus conquered death and paid mankind's sin debt.

- **Red Line Connection:** Jesus Christ is the fulfillment of God's promised Savior of the world. Background Passage: Matthew 27:27 to 28:8

- **Focal Passages:** Matthew 27:35–46; 28:1–8

133

Questions to Consider:

1. What were the sayings of Jesus on the Cross?

2. How would you describe the scene from the perspective of standing at the foot of the Cross? What might have been the sights and sounds at the Crucifixion?

3. How was prophecy fulfilled in Jesus' death and resurrection?

4. What does the empty tomb mean to you?

Jesus' Last Days on Earth

Red Line Verse: *"Were not our hearts burning within us while He was speaking to us on the road, while He was explaining the Scriptures to us?"* (Luke 24:32)

Red Line Statement: After His resurrection, Jesus appeared to many people and helped them understand why He had suffered and died for their sins.

Red Line Connection: Many eyewitnesses testified of the risen Jesus.

Focal Passage: Luke 24:13–35

Questions to Consider:

1. When did this conversation take place? Read Luke 24:1–12 to learn about the events that had already taken place that day.

2. What did Cleopas seem to understand about Jesus the Messiah? What did he not understand?

3. Before revealing Himself as the risen Messiah, Jesus shared the good news with these two disciples another way; what did Jesus do first (v. 27)?

4. How can you personally relate to the two disciples in this story?

SAMPLE LESSON FROM
THIN RED LINE VOLUME 4

LIFE LESSON 48

GOD IS AT WORK, EVEN IN OUR UNCERTAINTY

Red Line Verse: *Some were being persuaded by the things spoken, but others would not believe.* Acts 28:24

Red Line Statement: Despite the perilous adventures of his long trip to Rome and his house arrest there, Paul shared the gospel message to Jews and Gentiles alike during his imprisonment in Rome; some people believed the gospel while others rejected Christ.

Red Line Connection: Paul was a faithful witness to Christ even during his days of arrest, and both Jews and Gentiles were able to hear the gospel message.

Focal Passage: Acts 28

 Listen Attentively to the Lesson

1. Tell the story of Acts 28 in your own words.

   Context: Paul was arrested during a season of ministry in Jerusalem (21:26–36). This arrest led to two years of imprisonment in Caesarea under Felix (24:27). When Festus succeeded Felix as governor, Festus examined Paul under questioning, and Paul appealed for the right to plead his case before Caesar (25:1–12). King Agrippa and Bernice visited with Festus not long after Paul had made this plea, and Festus required Paul to stand before them and explain his arrest.

King Agrippa was not impressed with the charges against Paul and said, "This man might have been set free if he had not appealed to Caesar" (26:32). Had Paul ruined his opportunity to be set free by appealing to Caesar? Paul had no reason to fret because the Lord had already revealed His plan to him: "Take courage; for as you have solemnly witnessed to My cause at Jerusalem, so you must witness at Rome also" (23:11).

2. Reconstruct Acts 28 together, including as many details as your small-group remembers.

3. Read the passage aloud together from Scripture, confirming the facts of the story. Amend any details suggested by small-group members that did not accurately represent the Scripture.

Investigate the Facts of the Lesson

Use these questions to guide small-group members to investigate the facts of this passage.

1. On Malta, how did the people of the island judge Paul (vv. 4–6)?

    They judged whether Paul was a worthy man based on appearances and what was happening to him.

2. When God used Paul to heal Publius's father, what resulted from this miracle (vv. 8–10)?

    Word spread and the other sick people on the island came to Paul and were healed. The islanders honored Paul and his men and gave them provisions as they departed. The writer Luke doesn't tell us if any of the islanders believed in Christ, but Paul's character suggests that he probably was a bold witness as he healed people. Consistently, God's manner of working through the Book of Acts was to allow the apostles to perform miracles to draw people to Christ. However, we can't be certain of how Malta responded spiritually to the power of Christ.

3. How long did Paul wait before taking his first action upon arriving at Rome (v. 17)? What was Paul's motive for this first action? Was Paul taking care of his own personal needs?

   Paul waited only three days to call together the Jewish leaders of Rome. He wasn't focused on his house arrest or his personal needs; Paul was focused on the cause of Christ and why God had brought him to Rome.

4. What strategy did Paul use to share the gospel with the Jewish leaders (v. 23)? What were the results (v. 24)?

   Paul preached through the Old Testament, pointing out how God's thin red line pointed to Jesus Christ. Some were persuaded, while others didn't believe.

5. What was the ministry that God provided for Paul while he was in Rome (vv. 30–31)?

   God prompted people to go to Paul while he was under house arrest, and Paul continued to preach and teach about Jesus Christ.

6. What other details do you see in this passage?

   Allow your small group to share other details that stand out to them and discuss the significance of each point.

 Find the purpose of the lesson

   Use these questions to guide small-group members to discover God's purpose for the passage.

1. God had a plan for Paul to go to Rome (23:11), but on Malta, Paul unexpectedly suffered a viper bite (Acts 28:3–5).

   a. Paul wasn't injured by the viper bite; what does this show you about God's determination for His plan to be completed?

      This viper bite was a surprise to Paul, but not to God! God's plan for Paul to reach Rome wasn't going to be ruined by anyone or anything, but that didn't mean that Paul wouldn't possibly suffer along the way.

b. Unexpected problems may also come your way. Will these trials interfere with God's ultimate plan for you? When you are uncertain about your future, is God uncertain?

We may feel sometimes as though trials are thwarting our progress. When we focus on circumstances and link God's goodness and love for us with how good or bad our circumstances seem to be, we might be easily discouraged and feel defeated when trials arise. God is always at work, and nothing that this world or Satan throws at us will ruin God's perfect plan for us. Our faith can be certain even when our path seems uncertain.

2. As Paul journeyed through Italy toward Rome, he was met by fellow Christians (vv. 13–15).

a. What did these Christians have in common with Paul? Why would they offer hospitality and go out of their way to encourage Paul?

They had a common bond through the blood of Jesus Christ. Their hospitality and extra efforts to meet with Paul were expressions of how Christ's love compels us to serve others.

b. To whom do you offer encouragement and hospitality? Who offers you encouragement and hospitality?

As your small group shares, be sensitive to anyone in your small group who perhaps has not yet experienced encouragement and hospitality in a personal way from your small group. Is there a small-group member who needs to receive some expressions of God's love from the group?

c. What did the visit from the brethren do for Paul (v. 15)? Share about a time when Christian brothers and sisters encouraged you.

Paul thanked God and took courage. The love of other Christians is a gift from God and especially a blessing when we're facing days of uncertainty like Paul was.

3. Before launching into the gospel, Paul explained to the Jews in Rome who he was and why he was under arrest (vv. 17–20).

a. What was Paul's understanding about why he was in chains (v. 20)?

Paul believed he was in chains for the sake of the hope of Israel.

b. What are you doing or experiencing for the hope of the nations, or for the hope of the lost around you?

Be prepared to share your own response.

c. The Jews' understanding was that Christianity was spoken against everywhere, yet they were eager to hear the gospel message from Paul, a Jew who had converted to Christianity (v. 22). Jesus Christ is still today one of the most controversial figures of human history, and much of the world renounces Christ. Why are people still interested to hear the gospel?

God's truth is compelling and the Holy Spirit is at work. God continues to draw people unto Himself in the hostile environment of this world. When Christians are willing to display God's love, grace, and power, the light of Christ shines brightly.

4. When the Jewish leaders of Rome disputed about the gospel, Paul left them with a final word from Isaiah 6:9–10 (vv. 26–27). Since Paul realized this prophecy was being fulfilled, why would Paul bother to witness to the Jews? Knowing that many people reject Christ today, why should we continue to share our faith?

Because of Isaiah 6:9–10, Paul knew not to be disillusioned in his ministry when Jews rejected the gospel. He remained faithful to share with them out of obedience to God's instructions, not knowing who would accept or reject Christ. We also share out of obedience, leaving the results to God. Some will reject Christ, but some will be persuaded.

5. What other truths from this passage stand out to you? What can we learn about God or learn about being a follower of Christ?

Allow everyone to respond. Share any other points of spiritual growth that the Holy Spirit brings to your attention.

Experience the Truth of the Lesson

Use these questions to allow God's transformational truths to reshape your hearts and minds.

1. When Paul arrived in Rome, he wasn't focused on his uncertain future or the threat of death; instead he was focused on whatever number of days he had left to do the will of God. Paul wasn't focused on what he *couldn't* do because of his house arrest; he was focused on what he *could* do, even though his movement was limited. What is your focus? Are you dwelling on what you can't do or what you can do?

   Challenge your small-group members to think about their attitudes and mindsets. Are they focused on the negative or positive? Are they operating under the guidelines of what they're able to do or being paralyzed with regret over what they aren't able to do?

2. In some respects, God helped Paul stay focused on what He wanted him to do and where He wanted him to be by having Paul under house arrest in Rome. Paul had proven that he was willing to go anywhere to preach the gospel, but at this stage of his life, God wanted him to stay in one place and be faithful to share the gospel with the people who would come to him at his home in Rome. Are you willing to go wherever—whenever—to share the gospel? And are you willing to stay in one place or remain in one ministry, being faithful to share the gospel?

   Talk about the importance of complete surrender to the call of Christ.

Between the Lines: Truth Points

Malta (v. 1)—literally, *refuge;* an island approximately 50 miles southwest of Sicily.

Us (v. 2)—Paul was traveling with other prisoners and Roman soldiers, but his personal traveling companions included Luke, the author of the Gospel of Luke and Acts, and Aristarchus (27:2).

Twin Brothers (v. 11)—In Greek mythology, the twin sons of Zeus, Castor and Pollux, were believed to be guardians of sailors. Roman sea vessels often bore the image of Castor and Pollux, the Twin Brothers.

The Market of Appius and Three Inns (v. 15)—Upon arriving on land at Puteoli (v. 13), the men began traveling along what is known as the Appian Way, an important road that extended from Rome to eventually reach the southeast coast of Italy. The Market of Appius (or Appii Forum) was approximately 40 to 50 miles out from Rome, and the town of Three Inns (or Three Taverns) was about ten miles closer.

Appeal to Caesar (v. 19)—Refer to Acts 25:11.

> *If I could hear Christ praying for me in the next room, I would not fear a million enemies. Yet, distance makes no difference. He is praying for me.*
> ROBERT M. MCCHEYNE

New Hope® Publishers is a division of WMU®, an international organization that challenges Christian believers to understand and be radically involved in God's mission. For more information about WMU, go to wmu.com. More information about New Hope books may be found at NewHopeDigital.com. New Hope books may be purchased at your local bookstore.

Use the QR reader on your
smartphone to visit us online at
NewHopeDigital.com

If you've been blessed by this book, we would like to hear your story.
The publisher and author welcome your comments and
suggestions at: newhopereader@wmu.org.

FOR MORE

"THIN RED LINE" SERIES RESOURCES, GO TO:

http://www.newhopedigital.com/ThinRedLine

WorldCrafts^{SM} develops sustainable,
fair-trade businesses among impoverished people
around the world.

The WorldCrafts Support Freedom campaign
actively empowers WorldCrafts buyers and
aids artisans by highlighting those groups involved
in human trafficking and sexual exploitation.

Learn more about the campaign, purchase products
in the campaign, download our prayer guide,
and learn how to mobilize others by going to
WorldCrafts.org/SupportFreedom.asp.

WORLDCRAFTS^{SM}
Committed. Holistic. Fair Trade.
WorldCrafts.org 1-800-968-7301

WorldCrafts is a division of WMU®.

Bible Study On the Go!

Interact. Engage. Grow.

New Hope Interactive is a new digital Bible study platform that allows you to unlock content to download your favorite New Hope Bible study workbooks on your tablet or mobile device. Your answers and notes are kept private through a profile that's easy to create and FREE!

Perfect for individual or small group use!

To learn more visit NewHopeInteractive.com/getstarted

Penny Stocks:
The Next American Gold Rush